# Golden Key and Silver Chain

# Golden Key and Silver Chain

## ... And 30 Other Bible-Based Meditations

Series # 12

Roger Ellsworth

First Edition: 2018

ISBN: 978-0-9600203-2-4

20181115LS

Great Writing Publications
www.greatwriting.org
Taylors, SC

www.greatwriting.org

# Purpose

*My Coffee Cup Meditations* are short, easy-to-read, engagingly presented devotions based on the Bible, the Word of God. Each reading takes a single idea or theme and develops it in a thought-provoking way so that you are inspired to consider the greatness of God, the relevance of the good news of the life, death, resurrection, and coming-again of Jesus, and are better equipped for life in this world and well prepared for the world to come.

www.mycoffeecupmeditations.com

https://www.facebook.com/MyCoffeeCupMeditations/

# Dedication

To

Hunter Martin

# About This Book

This book is the result of the labors Roger Ellsworth and the thought he has given to various passages of Scripture over the years. You may read more about Roger on page 141.

We hope you will enjoy these Bible-based meditations. We would love to hear from you, so please send us a note to tell us what you think—which ones you liked most, and how they made a difference in your life or in the life of a family member, friend, or work associate. To reach us online, go to www.mycoffeecupmeditations.com/contact

# MY COFFEE-CUP

# MEDITATIONS

# Table of Contents

**Ten Crucial Promises**

# The App

www.mycoffeecupmeditations.com

Be sure you get the app!

# -1-

## From God's Word, the Bible...

*"You search the Scriptures, for in them you think you have eternal life; and these are they which testify of Me."*

*John 5:39*

# Golden Key and Silver Chain

There's a golden key that unlocks the Bible. That key is Jesus. He tells us so. On the day of His resurrection, He met two travelers on the road to Emmaus and "expounded to them in all the Scriptures the things concerning Himself" (Luke 24:27).

There you have it! Jesus believed that all the Old Testament Scriptures concerned Him. Later that day, He met His disciples in Jerusalem and assured them "that all things must be fulfilled which were written in the Law of Moses and the Prophets and the Psalms concerning Me" (Luke 24:44).

To say the Old Testament is not about Jesus is to quarrel with Jesus. That's an unwinnable quarrel.

So Jesus identifies Himself as the key to the Bible. He is its grand subject. In the Old Testament, He is promised. In the New Testament, He is presented.

I am calling this the golden key because we associate gold with enormous value, and there's nothing more valuable than the Bible's presentation of Jesus. There is no greater knowledge to be had than the knowledge of Christ. There are no greater riches to be possessed than the riches of Christ.

The Bible will be to us as a heavy, steel door if we don't insert into its lock the golden key.

It is fascinating to read the Old Testament with the Lord Jesus in mind. Its main characters picture Him, as do its main events. In addition to those characters and events, the Old Testament also offers many explicit promises about Him and His redeeming work. We might say that the Old Testament gives us a chain of people, events, and promises on which the golden key hangs—let's call it a silver chain. A golden key on a silver chain—that's double value! There is inestimable value in Christ, and there is incalculable value in the people, events, and promises that point to Him.

The devotions that follow will deal with some of these people, events, and promises. We will look at ten crucial people, ten crucial pictures (events), and ten crucial promises (prophecies).

These devotions have both believers and unbelievers in mind. My hope for those who believe in Christ is that they will be thrilled and moved to greater worship of Christ and service to Him.

I've been concerned for several years now about believers in Christ falling into the clutches of dull familiarity. That can easily happen. Many of us have been familiar with the glorious truth of Christ for a long time. What a blessing! But our blessing becomes a problem if we let our familiarity with Christ dull our appreciation of Him. Familiarity with glorious truth can put us in the camp of the Ephesian Christians who "left" their first love (Rev. 2:4).

Getting a fresh sight of Christ will go a long way toward helping us love Him as we should, and examining the various links of the silver chain in the Old Testament is one way to get a fresh sight of Him. So, I invite my fellow-believers to join me in looking for the Lord Jesus in various Old Testament people, types, and promises. As we do, let's make this our prayer:

*Let me love Thee more and more,*
*Till this fleeting, fleeting life is o'er;*
*Till my soul is lost in love,*
*In a brighter, brighter world above.*
(Fanny J. Crosby)

I also hope that people who have not yet come to faith in Christ who pick up this book will read enough to be amazed to learn how consistently and completely Jesus is presented in the Old Testament.

Many unbelievers reject Christ because they assume there is insufficient evidence for Him. They enjoy projecting themselves as being so intelligent that they can't be duped by believing in One for whom there is little or no evidence. And they assume that those who do believe in Him are in the clutches of ignorance and superstition. They would be shocked to know that many Christians—who once assumed that there is no evidence for Christ—began to study the evidence and took Him as their Savior.

The truth about the skeptics is this: they reject Christianity, not because of a lack of evidence, but rather because they don't want to go where the evidence leads.

My invitation to believers and unbelievers is the same: come with me, look for Jesus, and be amazed.

# -2-

# From God's Word, the Bible...

*"For God knows that in the day you eat of it your eyes will be opened, and you will be like God, knowing good and evil."*

*Genesis 3:5*

# Adam, the Representative Head

We now begin to consider ten people of the Old Testament who picture the Lord Jesus. The first of these is Adam. The human story is the story of two heads. There have only been two. There will never be another. The first head represented the whole human race. That was Adam. The second head represents a new race.

Our first head plunged us all into sin and ruin. Yes, what Adam did counted for us all. God made Adam in His own image and placed him in the garden of Eden with only one commandment. He was not to eat of the tree of knowledge of good and evil.

Adam failed to keep that commandment. He and Eve yielded to the devil's temptation and ate the forbidden fruit.

That act of disobedience counted for us all. Adam's sin was my sin. Adam's sin was your sin. Since his sin was ours, the penalty for it was also ours. What was the penalty for Adam's sin? Death! Not just physical death, but also spiritual and eternal death! Adam didn't die physically on the same day that he disobeyed God, but he did die. He died spiritually that day. He was alienated from God. His mind, which was made to understand the truth of God, was now darkened. His affections, which were made to love God, were now degraded. His will, which enabled him to seek after God, was now deadened.

And the spiritual death that he died that day would bring in its wake both physical and eternal death. The greatest calamity that has ever occurred in all of human history is the first calamity—the one that occurred when Adam disobeyed God.

Many object to this matter of Adam being our representative head. They insist that it wasn't right or fair for God to let Adam represent all of us, as if God doesn't have the right to do with His creatures as He wills!

But the Bible is so plain on Adam's representation that to deny it is to announce that we don't really believe the Bible or accept it as our authority. The Apostle Paul states it very clearly in these words: ". . .through one man sin entered the world and death through sin. . ." (Rom. 5:12). He also says ". . . by the one man's offense many died" (Rom. 5:15).

Paul made similar statements in Romans 5:17, 18 and 19 and also in 1 Corinthians 15:22. Please note in Romans 5 the steady drumbeat of the phrase "one man." That one man was Adam. There can be no doubt about that.

Those who object to the teaching of Adam's headship should ponder why it is that we all sin and we all die. Those who want to disprove Adam's headship can do so if they stop sinning and stop dying. The fact that they can't do so should make them more receptive to what the Bible says about Adam.

God could have left us all under Adam as our head. He was under no obligation to lift us from the sin and death that

Adam brought upon us. But God's grace caused Him to pity us and to provide a way of escape from our sin and death.

What did God do? He appointed another representative head—His Son, the Lord Jesus Christ. Jesus came to this earth to succeed where the first Adam failed. He came to be the second and last Adam. To fill this role, Jesus had to take our humanity. He did that when He was born to Mary in Bethlehem. But in taking our humanity, He didn't divest Himself of His deity.

Was the first Adam tempted to sin? So was Jesus (Matt. 4:1-11). But He didn't yield to temptation.

If Adam as our representative head had obeyed God and refused to yield to temptation, he would have secured for all of us right standing with God. He failed. But Jesus, by His perfect obedience, secured for all who believe in Him the righteousness that God demands.

After living that perfect life, Jesus, the second Adam, went to the cross to die a special death. He received on that cross the penalty for sinners. In addition to depriving us of the righteousness we need, Adam's sin had brought upon us the penalty that must be paid before we can ever be accepted by God. That penalty is death in all its forms. Jesus endured that death on the cross.

So Jesus by His life provided the righteousness we need, and by His death paid the penalty.

Adam's failure as the first head cried out for the head of a redeemed race. In Jesus we have that head.

# -3-

# From God's Word, the Bible...

"I will make you a great nation;
I will bless you
And make your name great;
And you shall be a blessing.
I will bless those who bless you,
And I will curse him who curses you;
And in you all the families of the earth shall be blessed."

Genesis 12:2-3

# Abraham, the Promise-Receiver

There are three monumental men in the Old Testament, men who tower over all the others. They are Abraham, Moses, and David. Each of these three men points us toward the Lord Jesus Christ in various ways, as do many of the lesser Old Testament figures.

There are some obvious parallels between Abraham and Christ. As Abraham was chosen and called by God to fill an important role, so was Jesus. As Abraham sojourned as a stranger in the land God promised to give him, so Jesus sojourned as a stranger on this earth.

But I suggest that the main way in which Abraham points to Christ is in the promises that he, Abraham, received from God. When the Lord called Abraham to a new land, He fortified him with seven promises. Abraham would: (1) be made into a great nation (2) be blessed (3) have a great name (4) be a blessing (5) bring blessing to those who blessed him (6) bring cursing to those who cursed him, and

(7) bring blessing to all the families of the earth.

Where does the Lord Jesus fit into this? The Apostle Paul emphatically says that the very promises made to Abraham were made to Abraham's Seed, and he identifies that Seed as Christ. Paul writes: "Now to Abraham and his Seed were the promises made. He does not say, 'And to seeds,' as of many, but as of one, 'And to your Seed,' which is Christ" (Gal. 3:16). If the promises made to Abraham were also made to Christ, then Christ would:

- Be made into a great nation. That nation would consist of all those who belong to Him by faith in His redeeming work.
- Be blessed by the Father as He, Jesus, performed the work of redemption.
- Have a great name. Paul writes about this very matter, saying of Jesus: "Therefore God also has highly exalted Him and given Him the name which is above every name, that at the name of Jesus every knee should bow, of those in heaven, and of those on earth, and of those under the earth, and that every tongue should confess that Jesus Christ is Lord to the glory of God the Father" (Phil. 2:9-11).
- Be a blessing. It's true that Jesus has brought innumerable blessings on people in general and on His people in particular, but this promise may relate even more to people associating the name of Jesus with being blessed, saying something along these lines: "The truly happy and blessed people are those who know Jesus."
- Bless those who bless Him and curse those who curse Him. All individuals in this world are in one of two camps. They either bless Christ or curse Him, that is, they either accept Him or reject Him. Those who accept Him are blessed "with every spiritual blessing" (Eph.

1:3). Those who reject Him will eventually hear Him say: "Depart from Me, you cursed. . ." (Matt. 25:41).

▶ Bring blessing to all the families of the earth. Matthew Henry calls this "the promise that crowned all the rest." It's the Father's promise to Christ that the good news of His work would be widely disseminated. It tells us that while Abraham was to be the father of a nation, the knowledge of the Messiah wouldn't be limited to that nation. It's true, of course, that Jesus was born into the nation of Israel. But while He came *to* one nation, He didn't come *for* one nation.

Paul captures this promise in these words: "And the Scripture, foreseeing that God would justify the nations by faith, preached the gospel to Abraham beforehand, saying, 'In you all the nations shall be blessed.' So then those who are of faith are blessed with believing Abraham" (Gal. 3:8-9).

This doesn't mean that every single individual will be saved. It rather means the nations will hear the gospel, and the inhabitants of those nations who believe in it will be saved.

Those who are saved by the redeeming work of Christ will finally see the fulfillment of this promise. The redeemed multitude around the throne of God will sing to the Lord Jesus Christ:

> . . .*You were slain,*
> *And have redeemed us to God by Your blood*
> *Out of every tribe and tongue and people and nation.*
> (Rev. 5:9)

As we see Christ in the promises God gave to Abraham, we can already see much of their fulfillment. As we see that fulfillment, our faith in Christ should be deepened and our anticipation of the future heightened.

# -4-

# From God's Word, the Bible...

*Then Melchizedek king of Salem brought out bread and wine;*
*he was the priest of God Most High. And he blessed him and said:*
*"Blessed be Abram of God Most High,*
*Possessor of heaven and earth;*
*And blessed be God Most High,*
*Who has delivered your enemies into your hand."*
*And he gave him a tithe of all.*

*Genesis 14:18-20*

# Melchizedek, the King-Priest

The book of Genesis introduces us to Melchizedek, who was both a king and a priest. His name means "king of righteousness." Since he ruled over Salem (later to be called Jerusalem), he could also be called "king of peace" (Salem means peace).

While we know little about him, the author of Hebrews holds him up as a type of Christ (Heb. 6:19-7:1). Before we get into that, let's delve into a bit of history. This history has to do with Abraham rescuing his nephew Lot. As you probably know, Lot had moved to the city of Sodom (Gen. 13:1-13). Sodom was, at this time, one of five cities controlled by a king with the cumbersome name Chedorlaomer. Along with three other kings, for twelve years Chedorlaomer had demanded tribute from Sodom and other cities. Having gotten their fill of paying this tribute, the rulers of these cities finally rebelled against Chedorlaomer and his coalition.

That didn't sit well with Chedorlaomer and his associates. They marched against the five rebellious cities. When they came to Sodom, they looted it and took many of its citizens captive, including Lot.

Lot's capture caused Abraham to spring into action. Forming a coalition of his own, he pursued the army of Chedorlaomer, defeated it, and freed Lot and the other captives (vv.13-16).

The king of Sodom was so grateful for Abraham's intervention that he offered to Abraham all the goods that had been recovered.

Now we get to Melchizedek! Abraham refused the goods and chose, instead, to give a tithe to the priest Melchizedek (vv.18-24). So we're finally ready to ask this question: In what ways can he be said to represent Christ?

- While the Bible refers to Melchizedek as "king of righteousness" (Heb.7:2), he could only be an imperfect representation of it. In all of human history, there has only been one person who was perfectly righteous, and that was the Lord Jesus. God demands that same perfect righteousness of us, and we can't meet it. But God accepts the righteousness of Christ on our behalf when we receive the Lord Jesus by faith.

Jesus' death was also connected with righteousness as He received on the cross the righteous penalty that God had pronounced against sinners.

Christianity described in a few words is this: Jesus provided the righteousness we don't have and paid for the sins we do have. What He did applies only to those who trust in Him.

- While the Bible refers to Melchizedek as "king of peace" (Heb. 7:2), the very fact that Abraham was returning from a battle shows that Melchizedek couldn't produce perfect peace in his world. Jesus is the greater "king of peace" who will eventually create a world in which there will be no conflict.

- The fact that no genealogy is given for Melchizedek leaves the impression that he had no parents and that his life was endless (Heb. 7:3). While Melchizedek could only suggest or represent endlessness, the Lord Jesus actually possesses it. His priesthood, in which He represents sinners before God, will continue forever.
- Melchizedek pronounced a blessing upon Abraham (vv.19-20), and the Lord Jesus Christ, as the priest of His people, pronounces blessing upon them as well. All spiritual blessings flow to us, not because of anything we do to earn or deserve them, but solely because of the priestly work of Christ on our behalf.

Abraham responded to Melchizedek's blessing by giving him a tithe (Gen. 14:20). It seems to be very likely that Abraham saw Melchizedek to be a type of the coming Messiah, and that he, Abraham, responded in an appropriate fashion.

The king of Sodom had come to Abraham to offer him the spoils of the battle. Melchizedek came to Abraham to offer a blessing. Abraham refused the first offer and accepted the second.

We should see in Abraham's choice the option set before us. On one hand, we have the righteousness and peace pictured by Melchizedek and truly provided by Christ. On the other hand, we have Satan offering peace and joy that he can't actually produce. God calls us to accept Christ and reject Satan.

# -5-

# From God's Word, the Bible...

*Then the LORD said to Satan, "Have you considered My servant Job, that there is none like him on the earth, a blameless and upright man, one who fears God and shuns evil?"*

*Job 1:8*

# Job, the Righteous Sufferer

Job, who probably lived during the time of Abraham, was a righteous man who suffered horrible things. He is described for us as one who was "blameless and upright" and as one who "feared God and shunned evil" (1:1, 9).

But Job's righteousness didn't immunize him from suffering. In quick succession he lost his children, his servants, his possessions, and his health.

These calamities weren't the result of bad luck. Satan had come before God to allege that Job loved God and served Him because God had blessed him. Furthermore, Satan argued that if God were to withdraw those blessings, Job would turn against Him.

The book of Job challenges us to ask ourselves if we love and serve God for His own sake or just to get good things from Him. It compels us to ask ourselves if God is to us a means to get ends that we want or if He is the end that we want.

So God allowed Satan to test Job at this very point: would he continue to be upright even in the loss of children, servants, possessions, and health?

Job, of course, was unaware of what had gone on in heaven between God and Satan. One of the greatest values of the book of Job is its reminder that there is always more going on in our lives than we realize. The book doesn't urge us to abandon our reason. It does tell us that there are many things above our reason.

Job had faith in the coming Christ. That's clear from his tremendous statement of faith:

> *For I know that my Redeemer lives,*
> *And He shall stand at last on the earth. . . .*
> (Job 19:25)

But Job also pictures Christ for us in ways that he couldn't have fully understood. As we look at Job's sufferings, we must surely realize that the Lord Jesus was the greater sufferer. Jesus was the more righteous man who suffered greater things with a more willing spirit.

Jesus was more righteous than Job. While the book of Job declares Job to have been righteous, it never says he was perfectly righteous. With all of his goodness, Job was still an imperfect man who committed sins. Jesus is the only person in all of human history who never sinned. He was "without blemish and without spot" (1 Peter 1:19; see also 2 Cor. 5:21 and 1 John 3:5).

And Jesus suffered greater things than Job. We can't minimize the sufferings of Job. They were horrendous. But they could never come near what Jesus suffered. When Jesus' suffering is mentioned, we are often inclined to think of such things as the hostility of those who hated Him, the cruel mockery, the scourging, the crown of thorns, and the physical agonies of crucifixion. These were all very real and painful, but the worst of Jesus' suffering lay in Him becoming sin for us and bearing the wrath that our sins deserve. The worst of His suffering was in those awful hours from noon to three in which He was forsaken of God (Matt. 27:46) so those who believe in Him never have to experience that same forsakenness.

We can be sure that in this life we will never be able to plumb the depths of suffering to which Jesus descended on our behalf. Those depths will finally be revealed to us in eternity, and we will be amazed.

One of the things that should amaze us even now is that Jesus suffered willingly. Job wasn't exactly a willing sufferer. He complained to his three friends, Eliphaz, Bildad, and Zophar, that God wasn't treating Him fairly. When God finally speaks to Job at the end of the book, Job has to "repent in dust and ashes" (42:6).

Jesus, on the other hand, never complained about the suffering that was involved in His mission of redemption. He gladly shouldered the load on our behalf. In Hebrews 12:2, we read that "for the joy that was set before Him," He "endured the cross" and despised "the shame."

There was joy in that cross for Jesus. It was the joy of redeeming sinners. And He kept that joy in view as He suffered the horrors of Calvary.

There's much about Job's suffering that is beyond our ability to understand, but we can understand that it points us to the suffering of Jesus on behalf of sinners. While it's not usually right to rejoice over the suffering of others, we can and should rejoice in the suffering of Jesus because He willingly and lovingly laid down His life for sinners such as we are.

# -6-

# From God's Word, the Bible...

*The famine was over all the face of the earth, and Joseph opened all the storehouses and sold to the Egyptians. And the famine became severe in the land of Egypt.*

*Genesis 41:56*

# Joseph, the Savior

Joseph, the great-grandson of Abraham, points us to the Lord Jesus in some marvelous ways. He was greatly loved by his father, hated by his brothers, conspired against, sold, and tempted. But he remained faithful through it all. Each of these details finds a parallel in Christ. And there are also several more interesting parallels.

This reading focuses on the picture of Jesus that Joseph — as the savior of his people — provides for us.

After being sold into slavery in Egypt by his spiteful brothers, Joseph, through a series of almost incredible events, came to prominence there. We remember that he had predicted to Pharaoh that there would be seven years of tremendous abundance followed by seven years of harsh famine.

The years of plenty came, and Joseph used that time to store grain. He "gathered very much grain, as the sand of the sea, until he stopped counting, for it was without number" (v. 49).

When the famine came, the people soon ran out of grain and came to Pharaoh for relief. Pharaoh responded to them by saying: "Go to Joseph; whatever he says to you, do" (v. 55).

The famine was also "over all the face of the earth," so people from other lands began coming to Joseph who "opened all the storehouses" of Egypt (v. 56).

So, Joseph functioned as a savior. He saved people from starvation in a famine-ravaged time. In so doing, he serves as a type of another and far greater Savior, the Lord Jesus Christ.

When we come to the New Testament, we meet another Joseph—the one who was to be joined in marriage to Mary. This Joseph received a visit from an angel, who announced that Mary was to have a special son. The angel said: "Joseph, son of David, do not be afraid to take to you Mary your wife, for that which is conceived in her is of the Holy Spirit. And she will bring forth a Son, and you shall call His name JESUS, for He will save His people from their sins" (Matt. 1:20-21).

Jesus came to this earth to be a far greater Savior than the first Joseph. In what ways is Jesus a better Savior?

First, Joseph opened a temporal storehouse to meet a temporal need; the Lord Jesus opens the storehouse of salvation to meet a spiritual need.

The people of Joseph's time were perishing physically, and his storehouse saved them. But perishing spiritually and eternally is far worse than perishing physically. It is that condition in which we are separated from God because of our sins, that condition which will ultimately issue into perishing eternally. Jesus has a storehouse full of forgiveness for our sins! He has a storehouse of salvation!

Secondly, Joseph had authority to open the storehouse of Egypt; Jesus opens the storehouse of salvation on the basis of far greater authority.

The authority by which Joseph operated was Pharaoh's. The authority by which Jesus operated was God's, and it is to Jesus alone that God has granted authority to open the storehouse of salvation. No one else can do so. Jesus Himself said: "All authority has been given to Me in heaven and in earth" (Matt. 28:18; see also Acts 4:12).

Thirdly, While Joseph did great things to open the storehouses of Egypt, Jesus did far greater things to open the storehouse of salvation.

Joseph had to plan and to work diligently for a period of seven years to make sure that the storehouses of Egypt were full. He had to exercise constant oversight. What did it take for Jesus to open the storehouse of salvation? He had to take our humanity. He had to also live in perfect obedience to God. He had to go to the cross to receive the penalty of eternal wrath in the place of sinners. He lives today to intercede for all those who come to God through Him (Heb. 7:25).

Finally, while those who came to Joseph had to purchase their grain, those who come to Jesus are given salvation.

Salvation cannot be earned or deserved. It is free. Paul said to the Christians of Ephesus: "For by grace you have been saved through faith, and that not of yourselves; it is the gift of God, not of works, lest anyone should boast" (Eph 2:8-9).

When needy people came to Pharaoh for help, he said: "Go to Joseph" (v. 55). We who know Jesus as Savior do not hesitate to say to needy sinners: "Go to Jesus!"

# -7-

# From God's Word, the Bible...

*For your servant became surety for the lad to my father, saying,
"If I do not bring him back to you, then I shall bear the blame
before my father forever."*

*Genesis 44:32*

# Judah, the Surety

Joseph's cup had been found in Benjamin's sack. It had been placed there as the test Joseph had devised to see if his brothers would be willing to let Benjamin go into slavery in Egypt, as they had done with him.

Judah, the brother who had suggested that Joseph be sold to the Midianite traders (Gen. 37:26-27), now spoke to Joseph on behalf of his brother Benjamin. Judah had promised his father Jacob that he would serve as the surety for Benjamin. Now before Joseph, he acts as that surety.

A surety is one who stands good for another. Joseph's cup had been found in Benjamin's sack. Benjamin was, therefore, the one who was under Joseph's sovereign indictment. He was the one who was sentenced to serve as Joseph's slave, a sentence Joseph emphatically stated in these words: ". . .the man in whose hand the cup was found, he shall be my slave" (v. 17).

But Judah had pledged himself to be the surety for Benjamin. As Benjamin's surety, he, Judah, would become the slave of Joseph instead of Benjamin. Even though the cup had not been found in Judah's sack, he would bear the penalty for it. If the penalty were slavery, a slave he would be!

The plea of Judah was so powerful and moving that Joseph "could not restrain himself" any longer. He had to reveal his identity to his brothers (Gen. 45:1-3).

In standing as the surety for Benjamin, Judah portrays the Lord Jesus. He is the surety for His people (Heb. 7:22).

Benjamin needed a surety. Joseph's cup was found in his sack. There was no way to get around it. And we need a surety as well. We might say God's cup is found in our sacks. In other words, God has the goods on us. He has given us commandments by which to live—the Ten Commandments—and we have all failed to keep them. We are sinners. What is it to be a sinner? It is to refuse to conform to the commandments of God.

Is there any hope for us? The answer for Benjamin came in the form of his brother Judah, and the answer for us lies in the Lord Jesus.

There is no cup to be found in the sack of Jesus' life! He was completely without sin (1 Peter 1:19; 1 John 3:5), and was, therefore, free from the indictment of divine justice. He, Jesus, was free to go even as Judah was (v. 17).

But the heart of Jesus was such that he could not be content to let the sentence of God's judgment fall on those He loved while He Himself walked away. The heart of a surety beat inside Jesus! He submitted Himself to the sentence of divine judgment so His people could walk away from it. On the cross, Jesus took the place of His people. He received the wrath that was due them. He went to hell on that cross so His people will never have to endure hell themselves. He became for us a far greater surety than Judah was for Benjamin because He endured a far greater sentence. The Apostle Peter tells us that Jesus "bore our sins in His own body on the tree" (1 Peter 2:24). That tree, of course, was the cross.

If we would avail ourselves of the work of Christ, we must quit defending ourselves against God, admit that His cup is in the sack of our lives, and believe in the saving work of the Lord Jesus Christ.

When Judah stood as the surety for his younger brother, he didn't know for sure that he would be allowed to receive Benjamin's sentence. He must certainly have hoped that Joseph would be merciful and lift from both him and Benjamin the sentence.

It was different with Jesus. He left the glories of heaven and came to this earth will the full knowledge that He would indeed bear the sentence of His people. Knowing full well that there was no way to avoid the sentence, He moved relentlessly toward it, and, in so doing, took all His people from being slaves of sin to being children of God. So, we now say with the Apostle John: "Behold what manner of love the Father has bestowed on us, that we should be called children of God!" (1 John 3:1).

# -8-

# From God's Word, the Bible...

*So Moses came and called for the elders of the people, and laid before them all these words which the LORD commanded him. Then all the people answered together and said, "All that the LORD has spoken we will do." So Moses brought back the words of the people to the LORD.*

*Exodus 19:7-8*

# Moses, the Mediator

In the earlier reading on Abraham, I identified Moses as one of the three monumental men of the Old Testament. God used Moses to deliver the Israelites from bondage in Egypt. He used him to constitute them into a nation; He used him to serve as a prophet to the nation; and He used him to lead the nation.

In these various facets of Moses' life, we get glimpses of the Lord Jesus. Jesus delivers sinners from bondage to sin and Satan; Jesus constitutes His people into a "holy nation" (1 Peter 2:9); and Jesus is the prophet who declares truth to His people. Jesus leads His people.

There's another role that Moses filled, and in that role he supplies us with the best picture of the Lord Jesus. That role is mediator. A mediator is a go-between. Exodus 19 provides us one example of Moses serving as the mediator between God and the Israelites. God spoke to the people through Moses (v. 7), and the people spoke to God through Moses (v. 8).

Why did God deal with the Israelites in this way? Why didn't He speak directly to the people and allow them to speak directly to Him? By using Moses as His mediator, God was driving home this powerful truth: He is holy, and the only way sinners can approach Him is through the mediator that He has appointed.

One way that God demonstrated His holy character to the Israelites was by having boundaries set around Mt. Sinai so the people couldn't come near it or touch it (vv. 12-13, 23-24).

Some lightly dismiss Exodus 19. As far as they are concerned, God is not the way that He was in Old Testament times. He is now loving and kind instead of serious and severe.

But the Bible affirms that God never changes (Mal. 3:6). We're dealing with the same God today as the Israelites of old. He is as holy today as He was then, and the gap between God in His holiness and sinners in their sins is terrifically wide. Our sins have put us at odds with God and in conflict with Him.

We need a mediator! We need someone to come between us in our sins and God in His holiness. Can such a mediator be found? The glad answer of the Bible is this: "For there is one God and one Mediator between God and men, the Man Christ Jesus. . ." (1 Tim. 2:5).

Jesus is a far better mediator than Moses ever was. Moses was an imperfect mediator because he himself was a sinful man.

Jesus is the perfect mediator. As God Himself, He could perfectly represent God. He came to this earth as a human being, adding to His deity our humanity. Now He could also perfectly represent us. Jesus was the God-man, fully God and fully man at one and the same time.

Jesus came to this earth to satisfy God's holy demands and to enable us to meet those holy demands. God demands that we be perfectly righteous to enter heaven. Jesus met that demand as He lived a perfectly righteous life. God demands that our sins, which disqualify us from heaven, be paid for. Jesus met that demand as He died on the cross.

When God's justice looks upon the perfect life of Christ and upon His sin-bearing death, it has to relinquish its hold on sinners. Christ has fully met its demands. On the basis of what Christ has done, God can and does pronounce guilty sinners as guiltless. Through Christ, we who were in conflict with God are now at peace, saying with Paul: "Therefore, having been justified by faith, we have peace with God through our Lord Jesus Christ" (Rom. 5:1).

Augustus Toplady, having found peace with God through Christ, celebrated that peace with these words:

> *The terrors of law and of God*
> *With me can have nothing to do;*
> *My Saviour's obedience and blood*
> *Hide all my transgressions from view.*

The one who rests on the mediation of the Lord Jesus Christ doesn't have to live in fear and dread of having to meet the holy God. The terrors of the God of Mt. Sinai have yielded to the Christ of Mt. Calvary because Jesus is "the Mediator of the new covenant" (Heb. 12:24).

# -9-

# From God's Word, the Bible...

*Then Aaron took it as Moses commanded, and ran into the midst of the assembly; and already the plague had begun among the people. So he put in the incense and made atonement for the people.*

*Numbers 16:47*

# Aaron, the Atonement-Maker

Numbers 16 is the ghastly chapter with the glorious end. The ghastly part is the rebellion with which this chapter begins. This rebellion, led by Korah, Dathan, Abiram, and others (v. 1) was directed against Moses and Aaron, the God-ordained leaders of Israel.

It didn't last long. God put an end to it by opening the earth to swallow the rebels (vv. 31-33).

That would seem to have put an end to all opposition to Moses and Aaron, but, shockingly enough, it didn't. The very next day "all the congregation of the children of Israel murmured against Moses and Aaron" (v. 41). This shows us how deeply entrenched sin is in human nature.

Now we come to this chapter's glorious end. God had already begun to visit this further expression of rebellion with some sort of plague. Quickly discerning what was happening, Moses told Aaron to take fire from the altar, put incense on it, and "make atonement" for the people (v. 46).

The action that Aaron took provided atonement. It satisfied the wrath of God against the sin of the people. It took their sin out of the way so that they could be at one with God or at peace with God.

How did Aaron's action accomplish this? We must keep in mind that we have here the high priest of Israel coming between God and the people and offering incense to God. This satisfied God. We know Aaron's atonement was effective because "the plague stopped" (v. 48).

The glory of this chapter, then, is the glory of atonement. The word "atonement" means "the making of one" or "to make at one with." The people of Israel were not at one with God. Their sin had alienated them from Him. Before they could be at one with God, their sin had to be dealt with or God's wrath against their sin had to be appeased.

This episode provides us with a picture of ourselves. We all need atonement. We come into this world in a state of alienation from God. Although God created us, sin has kept us from being at one with Him.

And there's no way we can ever have that oneness until our sins are taken out of the way.

As Aaron made atonement for his people on that occasion, so Jesus has made atonement for His people. He did so by going to the cross. There he stood between the dead — spiritually dead sinners — and the living God. He was on that cross in the capacity of the high priest of His people. He offered himself on their behalf. He received God's wrath that was going out toward His people. In receiving it, He exhausted it. He didn't receive *some* of God's wrath so that His people would only have to bear the rest. He received it *all* so that they would have to bear none.

And as God the Father looked upon that cross and saw the flickering embers of what had been His holy wrath against sin, He was satisfied. That death was like sweet incense to Him. His nostrils had been filled with the stench of our sins and the burning of His own wrath, but the death of Christ was like a soothing aroma to Him. It replaced the stench. He smelled that aroma and was satisfied. This is why the Apostle Paul wrote these words: ". . .Christ also has loved us and given Himself for us, an offering and a sacrifice to God for a sweet-smelling aroma" (Eph. 5:2).

Henry Mahan moves from Aaron to Christ by saying:

The people were dropping like dust as Aaron stepped between them and God to plead God's mercy for them. He was in effect saying, "Death and judgement, you must march over me and my atonement; you must smite God's high priest and ignore God's atonement if you destroy the people." Wrath and judgement have a claim on us. Justice is ready to smite the sheep. But Christ, the Mediator, stands between us and the justice of God and says, "You must walk over me and ignore my blood to destroy my sheep. . . ."[1]

We should see in Aaron positioning himself between God's wrath and the people a picture of Christ putting Himself in the same position on the cross. And we should be thankful for that picture.

---

[1] Henry Mahan, *With New Testament Eyes*, Evangelical Press, 1993, vol. i, p. 68

# -10-

## From God's Word, the Bible...

*Then Samuel took the horn of oil and anointed him in the midst of his brothers; and the Spirit of the LORD came upon David from that day forward. So Samuel arose and went to Ramah.*

1 Samuel 16:13

# David, the Warrior, King, and Writer

You see in the title for this reading the three words that come to my mind when I think of David—warrior, king, and writer.

David was a warrior. There can be no doubt about that. He burst on the scene in Israel by defeating Goliath. But that was only the first in a long line of the victories he won for Israel.

David was Israel's great king, ruling over the nation with unusual skill and wisdom. Ask someone who knows his or her Bible to name Israel's greatest king, and he or she will probably mention David.

David was a writer, composing more than 73 of the 150 psalms. I say "more than" because he evidently wrote more psalms than the 73 that bear his name. Psalm 2 doesn't carry David's name, but the early church attributed it to him (Acts 4:25).

In each of his major roles, David serves as a picture of the Lord Jesus Christ. David's greatest victory as a warrior came when he defeated the nine-feet tall Philistine giant, Goliath (1 Sam. 17:1-58).

For many years, now, it has been trendy for Christians to look to this account for tips on how to defeat the "giants" in their lives. We do better if we see in this story a greater David defeating a greater enemy to achieve a greater deliverance. The greater David is the Lord Jesus. The greater enemy is Satan. And the greater deliverance is deliverance from sin and Satan through the salvation provided by Christ. The Apostle Paul affirms that believers have been "delivered. . . from the power of darkness" (Col. 1:13).

By the way, David defeated Goliath with a sling and a stone. What unlikely instruments! The Lord Jesus defeated Satan by an even more unlikely instrument—a Roman cross!

As the king over Israel, David pictured the kingly office of the Lord Jesus Christ.

Jesus' kingdom is not of this world. It is now spiritual in nature, as He rules in the hearts of His people (John 18:36-37). A day will come in which the kingdom of Christ will be openly and universally seen (1 Cor. 15:24-28; Rev. 11:15).

We can't think of David's rule over Israel without realizing how imperfect it was. He could have done a better job of managing the moving of the Ark of the Covenant (2 Sam. 6:1-15). He committed adultery with Bathsheba, had her husband killed, and attempted to cover up the whole sordid affair (2 Sam. 11:1-12:23). David mishandled his son Absalom to such a degree that it almost cost him his kingdom (2 Sam. 13:1-19:43). He conducted a census of the people, although God had strictly forbidden it (2 Sam. 24:1-25).

Each of these failings doesn't nullify or void David as a type of Christ. They rather show us that he was an imperfect type of Christ, and they should drive us to an even greater appreciation of Christ, who has been and is the King who never fails.

God Himself used David's kingship to point to the kingship of the Lord Jesus. God said to David: "And your house and your kingdom shall be established forever before you. Your throne shall be established forever" (2 Sam. 7:16).

The word "forever," used twice in that verse, carries us beyond David himself to the eternal realm. No earthly king or kingdom can last forever. But the kingdom of Christ will last forever (Luke 1:30-33).

As a writer, David didn't picture Jesus as a writer because Jesus left us no written works. But in his writing, David points us to Christ in psalms that are either indirectly messianic (18, 20, 21, 45, 69, 72, 89, 101, 132, 144) or explicitly messianic (2, 22, 110, 118).

David is one of the main links in the Old Testament chain that leads to Christ. As we have seen, he either pictures Christ or points to him. David was placed in a very unusual and privileged position. His son was his Lord! The Messiah would be his son in that he would be one of David's descendants. But the Messiah would also be his Lord in that He would be God in human flesh. David looked forward in faith to the coming Christ. What David eagerly anticipated finally came to pass when his descendants, Joseph and Mary, journeyed to his birthplace, the village of Bethlehem. There Jesus was born, David's son and David's Lord.

As King, Jesus is Lord, the mighty One who is able to save completely all who come to Him by faith. Is He your Lord and Savior?

# -11-

## From God's Word, the Bible...

*Then I said to them, "You see the distress that we are in, how Jerusalem lies waste, and its gates are burned with fire. Come and let us build the wall of Jerusalem, that we may no longer be a reproach."*

*So I sent messengers to them, saying, "I am doing a great work, so that I cannot come down. Why should the work cease while I leave it and go down to you?"*

*Nehemiah 2:17; 6:3*

# Nehemiah, the Builder

L et's review. Because of their sinfulness, most of the citizens of Jerusalem were carried into captivity in Babylon in 586 BC. After being the dominant world power for quite a time, Babylon had finally been conquered by the Persians. The Persian king, Cyrus, issued a decree that released the Jews from captivity and allowed them to return to Jerusalem.

Most of the Jews took advantage of that decree and made their way home. Some chose to stay in Persia. Nehemiah was one of those. He had a prestigious position there, serving as cupbearer to the king. Nehemiah seems to have been enjoying his life in Persia. But that changed when a delegation arrived from Jerusalem to lay before Nehemiah facts about that city's terrible condition. They described Jerusalem as being in "great distress and reproach," and added: "The wall of Jerusalem is also broken down, and the gates are burned with fire" (1:3).

This report caused Nehemiah great distress. It drove him to prayer and compelled him to ask the king of Persia for a leave of absence (2:1-6).

Upon arriving in Jerusalem, Nehemiah took the lead in rebuilding the wall. The work would be hard and long, and the difficulties and obstacles were probably more challenging and numerous than Nehemiah ever expected. But he and his workers persevered until the work was done.

Nehemiah makes me think of Jesus in a couple of very important ways. One is that he obviously had a heart for the work. He loved Jerusalem and yearned to see her flourish. He hated seeing her in such a low condition. Nehemiah understood how vital it was for Jerusalem to have a wall. For a city to be without a wall was "a reproach" (2:17). It was an embarrassment. It caused those around them to heap insults and scorn on them. It was also dangerous. The city without a wall was easy prey. Nehemiah's love for Jerusalem was such that he considered the building of the wall to be "this good work" (2:18).

Doesn't all of that make you think of Jesus? It should. The Lord Jesus loves His church even more than Nehemiah loved Jerusalem, and He is committed to building her. He said: ". . .on this rock I will build My church, and the gates of Hades shall not prevail against it" (Matt. 16:18).

The Lord Jesus considered the matter of building His church to be such a good work that He left the glories of heaven to come to this earth to build His church.

Building the wall of Jerusalem was a very costly venture for Nehemiah. He had to leave the comfort and security of Persia to face many threats. Building His church required Jesus to leave the glory and comfort of heaven to die a special death on the cross. That death was the means by which Jesus made the church His own and began building her. The Apostle Paul says: "Christ also loved the church and gave Himself for it" (Eph. 5:25).

That brings me to a second way in which Nehemiah makes me think of Jesus. Tobiah and Sanballat, a couple of unsavory fellows, opposed the rebuilding of Jerusalem's wall. They pretended to want to sit down and talk with Nehemiah, but he saw that their real intent was to do him harm (6:2). So Nehemiah refused by saying to them: "I am doing a great work, so that I cannot come down. Why should the work cease while I leave it and go down to you?" (6:3).

Jesus was on the cross to do a great work. He was there to provide salvation for sinners so they could be part of the church He is building. While Jesus was on the cross, the religious leaders of the Jews gathered round Him and said: "If He is the King of Israel, let Him now come down from the cross, and we will believe Him" (Matt. 27:42).

Those cruel mockers didn't realize it, but Jesus did indeed have the power to step down from the cross. But as Nehemiah refused to come down from the wall, Jesus refused to come down from the cross. He stayed there until He cried: "It is finished!" (John 19:30). Because Jesus refused to come down from the cross, we have salvation.

We should be thankful for Nehemiah and the glimpses that he gives us of Jesus, but we should be even more thankful for Jesus Himself. As the Apostle Paul once wrote to the believers in Corinth, referring to God's gift of salvation in Christ, "Thanks be to God for His indescribable gift!" (2 Cor. 9:15).

# -12-

## From God's Word, the Bible...

*And God said to Noah, "The end of all flesh has come before Me,*
*for the earth is filled with violence through them; and behold,*
*I will destroy them with the earth."*

*Genesis 6:13*

# Noah's Ark

Now we turn out attention to ten events of the Old Testament that picture Christ. We begin with Noah and the ark. I can't read the account of Noah in Genesis without thinking of these words from Hebrews 11:7—"By faith, Noah, being divinely warned of things not yet seen, moved with godly fear, prepared an ark for the saving of his household. . . ."

Noah lived thousands of years ago. He didn't drive a car, watch television, surf the Internet or send texts, but *there's a way that we are all exactly like Noah*. Noah was warned by God "of things not yet seen." Noah was told of judgment to come (Gen. 6:11-13). This judgment was to come in the form of a great flood. God warned Noah about this, and Noah warned others.

We have also been warned by God of judgment to come. Where is this warning? It is in the Bible. Even if a person doesn't read or believe the Bible, the warning is there. The Bible tells us that this world is not all that there is. It says: ". . .it is appointed for men to die once, but after this the judgment. . ." (Heb. 9:27, see also Rom. 14:12).

Judgment Day isn't going to be the same for everyone. Some will hear the Lord say: "Come, you blessed of My Father, inherit the kingdom prepared for you from the foundation of the world. . ." (Matt. 25:34). Others will hear these solemn words: "Depart from Me, you cursed, into the everlasting fire prepared for the devil and his angels. . ." (Matt. 25:41).

This isn't popular teaching. People want human justice and are outraged when criminals go unpunished. But they don't want divine justice. They want God to look past their sins as if those sins had never been committed. That amounts to wanting God to deny His own justice. This He will never do. Our only hope lies not in God denying His justice, but rather in His justice being satisfied as it pertains to us.

*There's also a way in which we cannot be like Noah.* Hebrews 11:7 tells us that Noah "prepared an ark." After God told Noah about the coming flood, He told him to build an ark. That ark would be the means of salvation for Noah and his family. The great storm that was coming would strike the ark, but it wouldn't strike Noah and his family because they would be safe inside the ark.

Is there an ark of safety to protect us from God's eternal wrath? There is! That ark is the Lord Jesus Christ. Noah's ark is a picture or type of Him. But there is a difference. Noah had to build his own ark, but God doesn't tell us to construct our own plan of salvation. Rather, He tells us that He has constructed it for us in His Son. All that remains is for us to get into the ark that God has provided for us—and more about that shortly!

How is it that Jesus is our ark of safety in the face of eternal judgment? When He was on the cross, God's wrath was on Him. Just as the rain fell and fell on Noah's ark but didn't fall on him, so on the cross the wrath of God fell and fell on Jesus. That same wrath will not fall on those who are in Him.

*There's also a way in which we should all be like Noah.* Looking once again to Hebrews 11:7, we see that Noah did what he did "by faith."

We can't build our own ark of salvation. God has already done that in Christ. But as Noah got into the ark to escape the flood, we can and must get into Christ in order to escape the judgment to come.

How do we get into Christ as our ark of safety? It is by faith. Faith is taking God at His Word. When Noah heard God's message about the flood that was to come and the ark that he was to build, He believed and acted. God has told us about judgment to come and about the ark He has provided for us in Christ. He now calls us to stop believing the foolishness of the world and to trust in Christ as our Lord and Savior.

# -13-

## From God's Word, the Bible...

*Then Abraham lifted his eyes and looked, and there behind him was a ram caught in a thicket by its horns. So Abraham went and took the ram, and offered it up for a burnt offering instead of his son.*

*Genesis 22:13*

# Abraham
# Offering Isaac

A braham knew Isaac had to live. Even though God had commanded him to offer Isaac as a sacrifice, Abraham knew Isaac had to live. The reason Abraham knew is because he had a promise from God. The promise was that he, Abraham, would have descendants through Isaac (Gen. 17:15,16). At this point, there were no descendants. If there were to be descendants, Isaac had to live.

So Abraham was caught between seemingly contradictory words. One word called for Isaac to live, the other for him to die. What was Abraham to do? Was he to believe one word and not the other? Was he to believe neither word?

Abraham solved the dilemma by believing both words. If God wanted him to sacrifice Isaac, he would, but he would also keep believing that Isaac would live. The author of Hebrews tells us that Abraham took into account that "God was able to raise him up, even from the dead" (Heb. 11:19).

So it was off to the mountain and up the mountain for

Abraham and Isaac (v. 2). We know how the account ends. Abraham didn't have to offer his son. Isaac was on the altar and the knife was in his father's hand when God intervened. Isaac wouldn't have to die because God determined that a substitute would die in his place. Nearby was a ram with its horns caught in a thicket. That ram would be the sacrifice instead of Isaac (v. 13).

Why? Yes, why? Why would God put Abraham through this experience? The answer is that God was taking Abraham to an even higher level of faith in the coming Messiah. God was preaching the gospel to Abraham on the day that he placed Isaac on that altar. God's command to Abraham to offer his son made Isaac a type of Christ. The author of Hebrews affirms that Abraham received his son from the dead "in a figurative sense" (Heb. 11:19).

God spared Abraham's son that day, but there would come a day in which God would not spare His own Son (Rom. 8:32). There was no ram in the thicket to offer when Jesus died. There was no ram with his horns caught in thorns when Jesus was hanging on the cross with the crown of thorns on His head. There was no ram for Jesus because Jesus was the lamb for us.

God went through with the sacrifice of His Son, and how we should rejoice that He did. Had He not done so, there would be no salvation for us. There, on that cross, God provided such a sufficient substitute for sinners that all who will trust in Christ will be forgiven of their sins.

We can be sure that Abraham came down from Mount Moriah that day with a light step and a happy heart. In addition to not having to offer his son, Abraham had received from the Lord a much better understanding of what the Messiah would do in the place of sinners. He must have kept repeating to himself what the Lord had said: "The LORD will provide." And provide God did. He sent His Son to this earth and to the cross, and, in doing so, provided salvation. It's not at all unlikely that Jesus' cross was placed on the very spot where Abraham built the altar of sacrifice for his son.

By the grace of God, Abraham understood that his personal salvation from sin and his entrance into heaven rested entirely on what God would do through the death of His Son. Abraham looked forward in faith to the coming and dying of Jesus, as did all the Old Testament saints, and he was saved. We must never think that God first tried one plan of salvation, then another and another. God has always had only one way of saving sinners. That way is His Son dying on the cross. Abraham saw that, believed it, and was saved. Jesus Himself said to the religious leaders of His day: "Your father Abraham rejoiced to see My day, and he saw it and was glad" (John 8:56).

If Abraham had known these words to be later penned by Ethel Taylor, he might have sung them as he and Isaac came down the mountain:

> *Calvary covers it all,*
> *My past with its sin and stain;*
> *My guilt and despair*
> *Jesus took on Him there,*
> *And Calvary covers it all.*

# -14-

## From God's Word, the Bible...

*Then he dreamed, and behold, a ladder was set up on the earth, and its top reached to heaven; and there the angels of God were ascending and descending on it.*

*Genesis 28:12*

# Jacob's Ladder

Jesus never hesitated to relate Old Testament stories to Himself. Jacob's ladder is one instance. When Jesus called Nathanael to be His disciple, He promised him that he would see "heaven open, the angels of God ascending and descending upon the Son of Man" (John 1:51).

Jacob had been a rotten fellow. He was a conniving scoundrel who had deceived his father and cheated his brother. If he didn't leave home, his brother, Esau, would probably kill him. So leave he did. He was headed to his uncle Laban's house in far-away Padan Aram (v. 5).

Before he left home, his father Isaac had pronounced upon him "the blessing of Abraham" (v. 4). As Jacob lay down on this particular night, those words may very well have been ringing in his ears. He was nothing at all like his grandfather Abraham, and here he was leaving the very land that had been promised to Abraham.

It must have seemed to Jacob that he pulled the plug on all of God's promises, and that heaven was forever closed to him. He was in for a surprise. As he slept, he saw a ladder extending all the way from earth to heaven with angels going up and down the ladder. And God Himself was above the ladder to give him a wonderful message of encouragement and comfort (vv. 12-15).

Jacob couldn't have complained if God had given him a very different dream—one in which there was no ladder at all between earth and heaven, one in which the gates of heaven were barred and chained with scowling angels as guards. God doesn't have to open heaven to sinners. He would be justified if He were to leave heaven closed and sinners in their sins. But God is also gracious, and, in grace, He has done everything necessary for us to enter heaven.

It's important to note that God revealed the ladder to heaven while Jacob was sleeping. That made it clear. Jacob could do nothing to earn God's favor. All he could do was receive that which God was revealing.

Jacob's dream speaks powerfully to those who are carrying a tremendous load of guilt, to those who assume that they have done such horrible things that there is now no way for them to ever enter heaven. There is a way to heaven! There is a ladder that reaches all the way from this earth to heaven itself. That way is Jesus. He is that ladder. Jesus Himself said: "I am the way, the truth, and the life. No one comes to the Father except through Me" (John 14:6).

How is Jesus the way to heaven? God demands that we be perfectly righteous and that our sins be removed before we can enter heaven. We don't have the righteousness God requires. But Jesus came to this earth in our humanity to live that life that we have refused to live. By His perfect life, He provided the righteousness that we lack.

What about our sins? There is only one way that they can be removed. The penalty for sin has to be paid. Jesus, who provided the righteousness that we don't have, also paid for the sin that we do have. He did this on the cross. There He received the wrath of God in the place of sinners so all those who repent of their sin and trust in Him don't have to receive that same penalty. Here it is in a nutshell for all who trust Christ—He got our sin, we get His righteousness. Paul tells us that God made Jesus "who knew no sin to be sin for us, that we might become the righteousness of God in Him" (2 Cor. 5:21).

How do we know that Jesus is the way to heaven? As we look at His life, death, resurrection, and ascension into heaven, we can see the angels of God ascending and descending upon Him, just as He promised Nathanael. In other words, as we look at Jesus, we can see the signature of heaven upon Him. It is there in the words that He spoke, in the miracles that He performed, in the prophecies He fulfilled, in the death that He died, and in the grave that He conquered.

Jacob was overwhelmed by his dream (vv. 16-17). We should be overwhelmed that God would open heaven to us through Christ.

# -15-

## From God's Word, the Bible...

*And the Angel of the LORD appeared to him in a flame of fire from the midst of a bush. So he looked, and behold, the bush was burning with fire, but the bush was not consumed.*

*Exodus 3:2*

# The Burning Bush

The incarnation of Christ, the crucifixion of Christ, and the resurrection of Christ all depicted in one desert bush! In a bush? Yes, in a bush! Stay tuned.

Moses was on the back of the desert tending the sheep of his father-in-law. There was such sameness about shepherding that it's safe to say that Moses wasn't expecting anything out of the ordinary on this particular day. But out of the ordinary is exactly what he experienced. A burning bush suddenly caught his eye and drew his attention. The mere fact that the bush was burning wasn't so extraordinary. It was rather the fact that the bush wasn't consumed by the fire. It kept burning and burning without being burned up.

As Moses drew near, the extraordinary bush became even more extraordinary. Moses could both see the Angel of the LORD in that bush and hear Him speak. We have here a miracle within a miracle. The first is the bush burning without being consumed. The second is the Angel of the LORD appearing in the burning bush.

We must not think that the Angel of the LORD was an ordinary angel, as if there is such a thing as an ordinary angel! The Angel of the LORD was actually the Lord Himself.

It's understandable that Moses wanted to get a better view of this bush (v.3). But as he approached, the Lord said: "Do not draw near this place. Take your sandals off your feet, for the place where you stand is holy ground" (v. 5).

The Lord calls us to reverence Him as we recognize His greatness and holiness. How we need to hear that call! In this day of easy, breezy familiarity with God, there seems to be little consciousness of how great God is and how unworthy we are.

The fact that the Lord stooped so very low to appear in a lowly bush pictures for us the incarnation of Christ. What was the distance between the glory of heaven and that desert bush? It must be about the same as the distance between the glory of heaven and our humanity. That is the distance Jesus traversed when He took our humanity.

The fact that the Lord appeared in the bush didn't mean that He ceased to be the Lord. And the fact that Jesus appeared on this earth in our humanity didn't mean that He ceased to be God. In coming to this earth, Jesus didn't subtract His deity. He added our humanity. He was still God even though He was in human flesh. The Apostle John put it in these words: "The Word became flesh and dwelt among us, and we beheld His glory, the glory as of the only begotten of the Father, full of grace and truth" (John 1:14).

The fact that the Lord was not only in the bush but also in "a flame of fire" pictures for us the crucifixion of Jesus. We might say that the Lord was in the bush so He could be in the fire.

Fire represents judgment. To say the Lord came to this earth to go through fire is to say He came here to go through judgment for us. That's exactly what He did on the cross.

Why was it necessary for Jesus to go through judgment for us? It was to keep those who trust in Him from going through that judgment themselves. Our sins deserve God's judgment, and that judgment is most fearful indeed—eternal separation from God. On the cross, Jesus went through the fire of God's judgment. He endured the fire of separation from the Father (Matt. 27:46).

The fact that the bush Moses saw wasn't consumed points us to a most glorious truth indeed—the Lord who was in the fire of God's judgment on the cross wasn't consumed by that fire. The cross wasn't the final word about Jesus. Yes, He died there and was buried, but He arose in complete victory on the third day.

When Moses saw the burning bush in the desert, he said: "I will now turn aside and see this great sight" (v. 3).

The Bible sets Christ before us—incarnate, crucified, and risen—and it urges each of us to turn aside from our sins and trust in His redeeming work.

# -16-

# From God's Word, the Bible...

*"Now the blood shall be a sign for you on the houses where you are. And when I see the blood, I will pass over you; and the plague shall not be on you to destroy you when I strike the land of Egypt."*

*Exodus 12:13*

.

# The Passover

The people of Israel had been slaves in Egypt for more than four hundred years when God moved to deliver them through the leadership of Moses. Pharaoh, the leader of Egypt, viewed the matter quite differently. Israelite slavery was so vital to the Egyptian economy that Pharaoh wasn't about to free the Israelites. He would need persuasion, and that's exactly what God provided for him by sending nine devastating plagues upon Egypt.

Pharaoh, being a stubborn fellow, still refused to release the Israelites. So one more plague was in order—the tenth and last plague. God was going to send His death angel over the land to slay all the firstborn. That sentence of death for the firstborn would have been carried out against the Israelites also if God hadn't made a special provision for them. But a special provision is exactly what God gave His people. If they would slay lambs, mark their doors with the blood of those lambs, and stay inside those blood-marked doors, they would be spared. The death angel would pass over them.

It all went according to God's script. The Israelites killed their lambs, marked their doors, and stayed inside their houses. The angel carried out his mission of death, sparing the Israelites while visiting Pharaoh and all the Egyptians. Having seen enough, Pharaoh decided to let the people of Israel go.

The Passover is a historical event with ongoing significance. It released the Israelites from their bondage in Egypt, but it also pointed those Israelites to an even greater Passover. That Passover would be their long-awaited Messiah, the Lord Jesus Christ. The Apostle Paul made this connection when he called Christ "our Passover" (1 Cor. 5:7).

Christians don't hesitate to call Christ their Passover because they know that through Him they have been saved from a far worse slavery, a far greater Pharaoh, and a far worse sentence than the Israelites of old.

Our greater slavery was the slavery of sin. Our greater Pharaoh was the devil himself. And our far worse sentence wasn't the physical death doled out by the angel in Egypt. It was the eternal death or eternal wrath that we stood to receive before Christ saved us. Paul neatly expresses it all when he says of Christ: "Much more then, having now been justified by His blood, we shall be saved from wrath through Him" (Rom. 5:9).

Just as putting the blood of those lambs on their doors saved the Israelites, so we are saved from eternal wrath by the blood of Christ.

Why does God insist on the shedding of blood as the way of salvation? It represents the pouring out of life in death. The penalty for sin is death. We can't have forgiveness if that penalty isn't paid. The shedding of blood in death means that the penalty for sin is paid.

When Jesus died on the cross, that is, when He shed His blood there, He was paying the penalty for sins so all who believe in Him will never have to pay that same penalty.

Perhaps someone is wondering how the physical blood of Jesus or His physical death could really pay for sin, which is spiritual in nature. How could Jesus' physical death pay for a spiritual problem? There are depths of meaning in His death that we can never fathom in this life, but we can say this: the physical shedding of Jesus' blood represented something far greater than physical death. His physical death was the outward and visible representation of something far greater than physical death. It represented Him being separated from God (spiritual death) and receiving the wrath of God (eternal death).

How could Jesus experience all that on the cross? We must always keep in mind that Jesus was a special person. He was God in human flesh—the God-man. So He could— and did—experience on the cross things that a mere man couldn't experience.

It's enough for us to know that the shedding of Jesus' blood saves all those who repent of their sins and trust in Him. If we want God to pass over us and not visit us in judgment, we must lay hold of the redeeming work of Christ by faith. It isn't enough to know that Jesus died on the cross; we must personally trust in Him in what He did there. The Israelites were not saved from death merely because they were Israelites. They were saved by blood. If we want God to pass over us on Judgment Day, we must trust in the shed blood of Christ, God's ultimate Passover Lamb.

# -17-

## From God's Word, the Bible...

*And Moses said to the people, "Do not be afraid. Stand still, and see the salvation of the LORD, which He will accomplish for you today. For the Egyptians whom you see today, you shall see again no more forever. The LORD will fight for you, and you shall hold your peace."*

*Exodus 14:13-14*

# The Crossing of
# the Red Sea

What a predicament! The people of Israel had been released from their slavery in Egypt and now had the Red Sea before them, and Pharaoh and his army behind them. There seemed to be no way of escape.

All of the Israelites were "very afraid" (v. 13). Some, in a terrific fit of illogic, concluded that they had been delivered from Egypt so they could die in the wilderness (vv. 11-12).

Moses assured the people that the Lord would fight for them (v. 14), and the Lord did. He commanded Moses to lift his rod over the sea (v. 16), and He promised that the sea would open as the people went forward (v. 15). That's exactly what happened. With a wall of water on each side, and with the ground under their feet being dry, the Israelites were able to get safely across. When the army of Egypt attempted to follow, Moses again stretched his rod over the sea, and those walls of water came crashing down on the Egyptians. To put it in a nutshell, God's people were saved and their enemy was destroyed (vv. 21-30).

The situation at the Red Sea seemed to be so utterly hopeless and impossible. But God made a way.

It makes me think of another seemingly hopeless and impossible situation. I'm referring to us in our sins. How can there be a way forward for sinners when their path is blocked by what appears to be an immovable barrier? That barrier was the Red Sea for the Israelites of old. For sinners, it is the barrier of God's justice. How is it possible for sinners to enter into the promised land of heaven when God's justice demands that they be forever barred from His presence?

The answer for us is the same as it was for those ancient Israelites—God made a way! The way God made for us was the death of His Son on the cross of Calvary.

If we could only get a fuller understanding of what took place on that cross, our hearts would leap for joy and our tongues fill with praise. On the cross, Jesus so satisfied the justice of God that He removed it as our barrier. Now the way to the Promised Land of heaven is open to us as the way to Canaan was opened when God parted the waters of the Red Sea.

How did Jesus satisfy the justice of God on the cross? He received there what that justice demanded—eternal separation from God! Imagine it! Jesus, in the space of the six hours on the cross—actually received an eternity's worth of separation from God. How can that be? It's all wrapped up in Jesus being a special man—the God-man. As such He was able to do on the cross that which no mere mortal man could do. As God in human flesh, Jesus was able to experience the wrath our sins deserve.

God's justice got its full due when Jesus died on the cross. God's justice can no longer block the way to heaven because Jesus has satisfied His righteous standards. It's important to remember that justice can only demand payment once. For justice to demand payment twice for the same offense would make justice unjust. That means this: since Jesus received on the cross the penalty for sin that justice demanded, those who are in Christ will never have to pay that same penalty.

So the great question is this: how do guilty, undeserving sinners get in Christ? And the answer is this: they do so by faith. To have what Jesus did on the cross count for us, we must come to the end of ourselves and trust completely in Him in what He did for sinners. Moses commanded the people of Israel to "stand still and see the salvation of the LORD" (v. 13). There was nothing they could do to save themselves. They could only trust in the Lord to save them. So it is with us. We can't earn our salvation or deserve it. We must rather take as our own these familiar words:

> *Nothing in my hand I bring,*
> *Simply to Thy cross I cling.*

The cross amounts to the crossing of the seemingly uncrossable. God's justice was the seemingly uncrossable barrier, but on the cross Jesus satisfied it or crossed it for all who believe. Those who trust in Christ will make it safely to their heavenly Canaan, never to be threatened again by the Pharaohs of this world.

# -18-

## From God's Word, the Bible...

*Then the LORD said to Moses, "Behold, I will rain bread from heaven for you. And the people shall go out and gather a certain quota every day, that I may test them, whether they will walk in My law or not. And it shall be on the sixth day that they shall prepare what they bring in, and it shall be twice as much as they gather daily."*

*Exodus 16:4-5*

# Manna from Heaven

The people of Israel were out of their bondage in Egypt and in the wilderness. How were so many people to be fed? God's answer was manna, which was "a small round substance, as fine as frost on the ground" (v. 14). It is further described as being "like white coriander seed" with the taste of "wafers made with honey" (v. 31).

God had a threefold purpose in sending the manna. The first, of course, was to feed the Israelites. The second was to test them. The Lord said: "Behold, I will rain bread from heaven for you. And the people shall go out and gather a certain quota every day, that I may test them, whether they will walk in My law or not" (v. 4).

This bread from heaven would be supplied on a daily basis. It would fall during the night and the Israelites would be responsible to collect it in the morning. The only exception to this was on the seventh day, the Sabbath. The manna would not fall on the night preceding that day. The people would, therefore, have to collect enough on the previous day to last them through the Sabbath (vv. 22-30).

The people of Israel had to trust God to send the manna each night and to send them enough to carry them through the Sabbath. Would they do so?

The passage tells us that many failed the test. Some tried to save enough manna for the next day (vv. 19-20). And some went out on the Sabbath to gather it (v. 27).

The third purpose of the manna was to point them to the Lord Jesus Christ. Jesus Himself made this connection with these words: "Your fathers ate the manna in the wilderness, and are dead. . . . I am the living bread which comes down from heaven" (John 6:49, 51a).

How did that ancient manna picture the Lord Jesus? Here are some answers:

- As the manna was sent from heaven, so was Jesus.
- as the manna was mysterious (v.15), so the Lord Jesus and his salvation are beyond human comprehension.
- As the manna was small and unimpressive in appearance, so was Jesus in his humanity.
- As the manna was a gift, not created by human toil, so it is with Jesus and the salvation he came to provide.
- As the manna was for every Israelite of every state and age, so Christ is the Savior for those of every state and age.
- As the manna was pleasant to the taste and satisfying to the appetite, so the Lord Jesus is pleasant and satisfying. (Everyone who has come to know Him has found Him to be sweet to the taste and satisfying to the soul.)
- As the manna had to be personally appropriated by the Israelites, so Christ must be personally and individually appropriated by faith.
- As the manna was sufficient for the people all

through their wilderness journeying, so the Lord Jesus Christ is sufficient for his people all through their pilgrim journey in this world.

▶ As the "mixed multitude" (unbelievers) in Israel despised the manna (Num. 11:4-6), so unbelievers despise Christ today.

No type of Christ is perfect. We must say, therefore, that while the manna prefigured the Lord Jesus in some ways, it falls short in other ways:

▶ The manna was physical food while Christ is spiritual food, food for the internal man.
▶ The manna decayed when kept; the Lord Jesus never decays.
▶ The manna was found only in the morning, but the Lord Jesus can be found at any time.
▶ The manna ceased when the people of Israel entered Canaan, but Christ will continue to be the manna on which His people will feed throughout eternity.

It isn't enough, however, to say that Christ is the manna for the Christian. We must also think about where the believer finds this manna. In other words, how does the believer feed on Christ? The answer is by looking into the Word of God where the Lord Jesus Christ is set forth.

Every Christian should take up the Word of God each morning so he or she can feed on the Lord Jesus. As we feed on the manna of the Word, we feed on the manna of the Lord Jesus.

# -19-

## From God's Word, the Bible...

*"Behold, I will stand before you there on the rock in Horeb; and you shall strike the rock, and water will come out of it, that the people may drink."*

*Exodus 17:6*

# Water from the Rock

Not long after the Israelites crossed the Red Sea, they came to Rephidim. It was to be the place of a problem and a picture. The problem was that there was no water for them to drink. The picture was of Christ.

Their thirst was severe, so much so that the people "contended" with Moses (v. 2) and "murmured" against him (v. 3).

The anger against him was so great that Moses cried out to the Lord: "What shall I do with this people? They are almost ready to stone me!" (v. 4).

The Lord was sufficient for the occasion. He told Moses to strike a certain rock. That striking would result in enough water pouring out to quench the thirst of the multitude (v. 6). That was the picture of Christ.

Are we really supposed to see the striking of this rock as a picture of Christ? The Apostle Paul thought so, writing these words about the Israelites under Moses: "For they drank of that spiritual Rock that followed them, and that Rock was Christ" (1 Cor. 10:4).

And Jesus likened Himself to water with these words: "If anyone thirsts, let him come to Me and drink" (John 7:37).

The thirst to which Jesus referred wasn't physical in nature. It was a burning thirst to have sins forgiven and to be right with God. Only Christ can quench that thirst!

How is it that the Lord Jesus is able to satisfy spiritual thirst? It's all due to Him being smitten as the ancient rock at Rephidim was smitten by Moses.

That's what happened to Jesus on the cross. There He was, in the words of the prophet Isaiah, "Smitten by God" (Isa. 53:4).

The Son smitten on the cross by His Father! Many despise the thought. They find it repugnant. They're right to say that God the Father loved His Son, but they're wrong to assume that love made it impossible for the Father to smite His Son. They fail to see that God's smiting of His Son didn't negate His love. It was rather because of His love for His Son and for sinners.

How did the Father's smiting express love for Jesus? In this way: through that smiting, God insured that Jesus would receive such great glory that every tongue will finally confess Him as Lord (Phil. 2:11).

Through enduring the Father's smiting, Jesus would receive far more glory than He would if the smiting had never occurred.

It was also the Father's love for sinners that led to the smiting of the Son. Jesus was on that cross in a special capacity. He was there as the substitute for sinners. He was their sin-bearer (1 Peter 2:24).

Because of our sins, we deserve the eternal smiting of God. Jesus took that smiting, so we don't have to endure it.

We must understand that God wasn't being cruel to Jesus when He smote Him for our sins. Jesus didn't have to go to the cross and receive that smiting. He did it willingly, and out of love for those for whom He died.

I don't hesitate to say, then, that God specifically commanded Moses to smite the rock in the wilderness so He could picture of the coming death of the Lord Jesus. How grateful we should be for that redeeming death!

Let's get back to Moses and the Israelites for a moment. Another time would come when those people would thirst again, and God would once more supply water for them from a rock. But this occasion would be different. Moses would be commanded not to strike to the rock, but rather to speak to it. And Moses, filled with anger and frustration, would strike the rock (Num. 20:1-13)

God was greatly displeased with Moses for doing that. The reason? God is very jealous of the types that He put in place of His Son's redeeming work. The smiting of the first rock was right because it pictured Christ being smitten on the cross. The second smiting was wrong because Christ was to be smitten only once for our redemption (Heb. 9:28).

The rock Moses was to smite seemed to be a very unlikely source for water, and the cross on which Jesus died seems to be a very unlikely source for spiritual life. But Moses' rock produced that water, and the cross produces that life. Christ is the greater rock who endured a far greater smiting to quench a far more serious thirst.

.

# -20-

# From God's Word, the Bible...

*"For on that day the priest shall make atonement for you, to cleanse you, that you may be clean from all your sins before the LORD."*

*Leviticus 16:30*

# The Day
# of Atonement

L eviticus is a cemetery for resolutions people make to read the Bible in one year. Many start out well. Genesis is so full of interesting stories that it's easy to get through. The first part of Exodus is the same. Things begin to get a little tedious toward the end of Exodus, but readers are able to persevere. For many it all comes crashing down in Leviticus, which seems to be such a hopeless jumble of rules and regulations.

One part of Leviticus will especially come alive if we properly relate it to Christ. It is the Day of Atonement, when Israel's high priest made atonement for the sins of the people.

The high priest had to follow the clearly defined procedure laid out by the Lord. This was not his atonement. It was the Lord's.

Here are some major ways in which the work of Christ is pictured or typified by the Day of Atonement:

- The high priest alone could perform all the work on the Day of Atonement. This pictures Christ alone making atonement for His people.
- The high priest putting off his regular garments, washing himself, and putting on white linen pictures Christ laying aside His glory and being clothed in our humanity in which He was undefiled by sin (Heb. 7:26).
- The two goats, one for the sin offering and the other as the scapegoat, are types of two aspects of the work of Christ. In addition to dying as our sin offering, He also bore our sins away to such a degree that they will never be found or remembered again (Heb. 8:12).
- As the burning of the skins and flesh of the animals used for sacrifice was to be done outside the camp, so Christ went outside the city of Jerusalem to be consumed with the fire of God's wrath (Heb. 13:11-12).
- One of the most interesting aspects of the Day of Atonement has to do with the Ark of the Covenant and the mercy seat. The ark contained the tables of stone on which God had written the Ten Commandments. Those tables represented the righteous demands of God. The mercy seat was set above the ark, and was exactly the same width as the ark. When the high priest sprinkled the blood of the sacrifice on the ark, it indicated that the blood of that innocent substitute perfectly satisfied the demands of God's law. That constitutes a beautiful picture of the cross of Christ. There Jesus shed his blood and perfectly satisfied God's demand for sinners to be punished for their sins. The law of God is perfectly satisfied by the cross of Christ.

While the Day of Atonement anticipated the work of

Christ, it could only do so in an imperfect way. Here are some ways that it came short:

- Israel's high priest offered the blood of an involuntary victim, but Christ is both our high priest and our sacrifice. In other words, He, as high priest, offers His own blood as the sacrifice for His people. And He did it voluntarily.
- While the high priest had to first make atonement for himself, Jesus, as our high priest, had no sin for which to atone. He was "without blemish and without spot" (1 Peter 1:19).
- While the high priest had to make atonement for the sins of the people each year, Jesus atoned for the sins of His people once and for all (Heb. 9:25-28).
- While Israel's high priest went into an earthly sanctuary to offer his sacrifices, the Lord Jesus went into the heavenly sanctuary to make His atonement (Heb. 9:11-15, 23-24), that is, He entered into heaven as our high priest on the basis of or by virtue of His shed blood.
- While Israel's high priest went into the Most Holy Place as the representative of his people, the Lord Jesus is both the representative and forerunner of His people (Heb. 6:20). In other words, He has, as their high priest, made it possible for them to follow Him into heaven itself.

Many things in the Old Testament point us forward to the Lord Jesus, but none more so than the Day of Atonement. Those people received pardon for their sins as they looked forward in faith to the Christ who would provide full atonement. We receive that same pardon as we look backward to the Christ who has provided that atonement.

# -21-

## From God's Word, the Bible...

*Therefore the people came to Moses, and said, "We have sinned, for we have spoken against the LORD and against you; pray to the LORD that He take away the serpents from us." So Moses prayed for the people.*
*Then the LORD said to Moses, "Make a fiery serpent, and set it on a pole; and it shall be that everyone who is bitten, when he looks at it, shall live." So Moses made a bronze serpent, and put it on a pole; and so it was, if a serpent had bitten anyone, when he looked at the bronze serpent, he lived.*

*Numbers 21:7-9*
*(Read the whole passage in Numbers 21:4-9)*

# The Serpent of Brass

Snakes! Lots of snakes! It would have been bad enough if they had just been ordinary snakes, but these were far from ordinary. They were "fiery serpents" (v. 6). Fiery serpents? Yes! Their bites burned like fire and caused death.

Where did these snakes come from? They came from God! They were His judgment on the Israelites for once again falling into the sin of complaining against Him. On this occasion, they complained about the manna with which God had been feeding them

It would seem that these people would have learned their lesson. The reason they were still eating manna is that they had grumbled about God requiring them to conquer the land of Canaan. God's judgment for that act of disobedience was to let them wander in the wilderness for forty years.

The fiery serpents certainly made for a terrible judgment. Many Israelites died from their bites.

But the same serpents that brought judgment also opened the door for God to display His grace and to point those people to the coming Christ. God's grace to the Israelites came in this form: He told Moses to make a serpent of brass, put it on a pole, and command all the people to look to that serpent for healing of the poisonous bites of those serpents. It was a matter of looking and living. So that's what those people did. They looked to the serpent on the pole and found healing. They could have refused to avail themselves of the cure because it seemed to be so absurd. Looking at a brass serpent on a pole would bring healing! There seemed to be no connection between that brass serpent and the real serpents. They could have refused the cure because it was set forth as the only cure. Imagine an Israelite saying: "Looking at this brass serpent is too narrow and intolerant. Because there aren't a dozen cures, I refuse to accept this cure."

There's no record of the people refusing the cure on such grounds. The impression we get is that they did as God commanded. They looked and they lived.

Many people these days would be quick to dismiss this as a very strange story that has no meaning for us. The truth is that there is tremendous meaning for us in this account. You and I are here. Just as those ancient Israelites sinned against God, so we have sinned against Him. We have broken His laws time after time (Rom. 3:23). And just as God pronounced judgment upon them, so He has pronounced judgment upon us—eternal death (Rom. 6:23; 2 Thess. 1:9-10).

And something else is in this old account as well. That is God's solution. The solution for those people was a serpent of brass on a pole, and the solution for us is God's Son on a cross. There should be no doubt about the brass serpent on the pole picturing Christ on the cross because Jesus Himself made the connection in these words: "And as Moses lifted up the serpent in the wilderness, even so must the Son of Man be lifted up" (John 3:14).

There are several points of connection between that brass serpent and the Lord Jesus. God's cure for the Israelites consisted of a brass serpent that was made like the fiery serpents. God's cure for our sins is His Son, who was made a man (John 1:14; Rom. 8:3; 2 Cor. 5:21; Phil. 2:7). That brass serpent had no venom, and the Lord Jesus had no sin (2 Cor. 5:21; 1 Peter 1:19; 1 John 3:5). The brass serpent was lifted up on a pole, and Christ was lifted up on a cross. The Israelites had to look to the brass serpent to be healed, and we must look to Christ to be forgiven of our sins. As that brass serpent was the only means of healing for the Israelites, Jesus on the cross is the only means of salvation for us.

That cross seems absurd to most people these days, but it is our only hope. Jesus went there to receive the judgment that we deserve. He went there to receive an eternity of wrath for the sins of all who will trust in Him. God's call to us is to stop dismissing the cross and stop debating about it. His call to us is to look in faith to that cross for our salvation. Look and live!

# -22-

## From God's Word, the Bible...

*"Therefore the Lord Himself will give you a sign: Behold, the virgin shall conceive and bear a Son, and shall call His name Immanuel."*

*Isaiah 7:14*

# The Promise
# of Jesus' Birth

The Lord Jesus is the theme of Scripture. He is the key to it, a gold key at that because He is of such enormous value. It can never be stressed enough that the entire Old Testament anticipates Him and His work of saving sinners. We seriously err if we think that God was trying first one plan of salvation then another during the Old Testament period. God has always had one plan of salvation, and that plan is His Son.

In the previous readings, we've concerned ourselves with people and events that point us to the Lord Jesus in one way or another. I'm likening those people and events to links in a silver chain, the chain on which we find the key of gold. The chain itself has value, but the key is of even greater value.

There are yet more links for us to treasure in the silver chain. Those links consist of the messianic promises of the Old Testament. These promises are numerous. They are also varied. In other words, they cover many of the details and aspects of the person and work of Christ.

Some of these promises pertain to the birth of Jesus. The prophet Isaiah gives us a very important detail about that birth. In the section of his prophecy that is sometimes called "The Book of Immanuel" (chapters 7-12), Isaiah informs us that Jesus would be born of a virgin (Isa. 7:14).

This promise was given to King Ahaz of Judah at a particularly tumultuous and threatening time. The Lord graciously chose to give Ahaz a sign that the threat of enemy nations would pass. A young woman, a virgin, would marry, conceive, and give birth to a son. While that child was still very young, the threat for Judah would pass. That was the meaning of Isaiah's prophecy for that time.

But in giving that promise to King Ahaz, God was giving a promise both of the birth of Jesus and the special nature of that birth. Jesus would be born, and He would be born of a virgin. The promise to Ahaz, then, had a larger meaning. How do we know it had this larger meaning? Centuries later, an angel would appear to a man named Joseph to inform him that the young woman he intended to marry was pregnant. That was no ordinary pregnancy. The angel said: "Joseph, son of David, do not be afraid to take to you Mary your wife, for that which is conceived in her is of the Holy Spirit" (Matt. 1:21).

That's not all the angel had to say. He proceeded to add that Mary's pregnancy was a fulfillment of the very prophecy that we have in Isaiah 7:14 (see Matt. 1:22-23).

The Gospel of Luke also affirms the virgin birth of Jesus. It informs us that "the angel Gabriel was sent by God. . . to a virgin betrothed to a man whose name was Joseph, of the house of David" (Luke 1:26-27). This virgin was Mary.

Gabriel appeared to Mary to tell her that she was to bear a son (Luke 1:31). She responded by asking: "How can this be, since I do not know a man?" (Luke 1:34). The angel answered by attributing her conception to the Holy Spirit (Luke 1:35).

The virgin birth of Jesus is often dismissed as being impossible. The angel who appeared to Mary dismissed those who dismiss it by saying: "For with God nothing will be impossible" (Luke 1:37).

God never takes kindly those who tell Him what He can and can't do!

Those who reject the virgin birth of Jesus would be well-advised to not set fire to the bridge over which they must cross to have salvation. If God couldn't do the virgin birth because such a thing was impossible, neither could He do the resurrection of Jesus, which would have been equally impossible. And the Apostle Paul emphatically asserts that there is no salvation for anyone if Jesus didn't come out of the grave. Paul puts it in these words: "And if Christ is not risen, your faith is futile; you are still in your sins!" (1 Cor. 15:17).

Jesus was born of a virgin, and His virgin birth was announced by the prophet Isaiah centuries before it occurred. What a marvel that is! But more marvelous than the promise of Jesus' birth is Jesus Himself, the One born to be the Savior of sinners.

# -23-

# From God's Word, the Bible...

*"But you, Bethlehem Ephrathah,*
*Though you are little among the thousands of Judah,*
*Yet out of you shall come forth to Me*
*The One to be Ruler in Israel,*
*Whose goings forth are from of old, From everlasting."*
*Micah 5:2*

*So they said to him, "In Bethlehem of Judea, for thus it is written*
*by the prophet:*
*'But you, Bethlehem, in the land of Judah,*
*Are not the least among the rulers of Judah;*
*For out of you shall come a Ruler*
*Who will shepherd My people Israel.'"*

*Matthew 2:5-6*

# The Promise of Jesus' Birthplace

The precision of the Old Testament prophecies of Jesus is staggering. We have an example of that precision in Micah 5:2. Little Bethlehem would be the place of Jesus' birth.

When did Micah offer this prophecy? Do you think that perhaps he was personally acquainted with Joseph and Mary, and in personal conversation with them learned that they were about to journey to Bethlehem so he sat down and wrote his prophecy?

Brace yourself. Micah lived more than 700 years before Jesus was born! The fact that Micah knew Bethlehem would be the place of the Messiah's birth shows us that there was more at work than Micah's brain when he wrote this prophecy. God was at work with Micah. God informed Micah that Bethlehem would be the birthplace of Jesus, and Micah put pencil to paper.

It's always been fascinating to me that God chose

Bethlehem as the place of Jesus' birth. Sending His Son into this world was a matter of such immense importance that we might expect it to have occurred in a prestigious city. But, no, it was Bethlehem.

Part of it had to do with the fact that Jesus was to be a descendant of David. What better place for David's greatest descendant to be born than the village where David himself was born?

Another part of it had to do with God's liking for the little. God loves the humble. He loves to yank the rug out from under men and women who strut around in pride and arrogance. The Bethlehem script offends such people. They always want God to do things in ways that rich, upper crust, highly intelligent, socially mobile people approve. God has a different agenda, saying:

*I will destroy the wisdom of the wise,*
*And bring to nothing the understanding of the prudent.*
(1 Cor. 1:19)

God's agenda is to go about His work in such a way that "no flesh should glory in His presence" (1 Cor. 1:29). Little Bethlehem would fill the bill; the grand cities of the world would not.

Those who hate the Bethlehem script think even less of the Calvary script. God sent His Son to this earth to die on a Roman cross so sinners can be made right with God and go to heaven. Proud people look with disdain upon that cross and say: "That's it? That's God way of salvation? What utter foolishness!"

But that foolishness, Paul says, is actually "the power of God and the wisdom of God" (1 Cor. 1:24). When God is being foolish, He is wiser than we are in our greatest wisdom.

That foolish cross provides salvation for sinners because

Jesus received there the wrath that those sinners deserve. Because He received it, they are freed from it if they will bow in repentance and faith before the One who died on that foolish cross.

Yet another part of God's choice of Bethlehem may have been due to His desire to demonstrate the vastness of the gap that Jesus had to cross when He came to this earth. From the glories of heaven and the company of angels to the tiny village of Bethlehem, a stall, and the company of Mary, Joseph, shepherds and animals! Could there possibly be a wider gap than that?

Something of the wideness of that gap is expressed right here in Micah's prophecy. Coming to Bethlehem is One who pre-dated Bethlehem! He is the One:

> *Whose goings forth have been from of old,*
> *From everlasting.*

Micah's prophecy came true. Jesus was born in Bethlehem. Only those with the most obsessive hatred of Christ would bother to deny that. But being born in little Bethlehem didn't make Jesus little. He would be "Ruler in Israel" (v. 2). That doesn't mean Jesus would be the political king of the political nation Israel. His kingdom is not of this world (John 18:36). Rather, Jesus reigns over the true Israel, spiritual Israel, that consists of all those who have come to the end of themselves and have come to faith in Him.

Bethlehem was certainly little in size when Jesus was born there, but His birth has made it big. It speaks about God fulfilling with precision a centuries-old prophecy. Put that single fulfilled prophecy along with all the other Old Testament prophecies fulfilled by Jesus, and you have the truth. The Jesus of Bethlehem is the Lord of glory who came to Bethlehem to take sinners to glory.

# -24-

## From God's Word, the Bible...

*For unto us a Child is born,*
*Unto us a Son is given;*
*And the government will be upon His shoulder.*
*And His name will be called*
*Wonderful, Counselor, Mighty God,*
*Everlasting Father, Prince of Peace.*

*Isaiah 9:6*

# Four Titles for Jesus

A lthough he prophesied many centuries before Jesus was born, Isaiah knew a lot about Christ. Those of us living on this side of Jesus' birth should know even more about Him, but that's often not the case.

As we arrive in Isaiah 9, we should be aware that we are still in that portion of Isaiah's prophecy that is often called the "Book of Immanuel." It's easy to find references to the coming Christ in this section.

I have no trouble seeing the Lord in the four titles that Isaiah uses for Him in Isaiah 9:6—Wonderful Counselor, Mighty God, Everlasting Father, Prince of Peace.

Yes, I'm aware that some regard Wonderful and Counselor as separate titles for the Lord. But since the other titles consist of two words, it makes sense to me to put Wonderful and Counselor together. When Isaiah looked down the corridor of time to see the Lord Jesus, he realized that He would be our Wonderful Counselor.

We associate counselors with keen wisdom and compassion for people.

Jesus isn't lacking in either of these essential qualifications. He is wonderful both in His wisdom and in His compassion. To say something is wonderful is to say that it evokes admiration and awe from us. Jesus is such a wise and compassionate counselor that we can only stand in awe of Him. He has perfect knowledge of both what is wrong with us and of what we should do with ourselves. His diagnosis is that we are sinners. His prescription for us is to turn to Him as our Lord and Savior. He offers this counsel to us because He cares so much for us. Wonderful counselor! That's Jesus! Wonderful in wisdom! Wonderful in compassion!

Isaiah also gives the coming Christ the title "Mighty God." The word "Mighty" carries us into the realm of warriors and war. Psalm 24:8 describes the Lord as being "mighty in battle."

As a mighty warrior, the Lord Jesus both delivers and defends His people. We aren't by nature the Lord's people. We come into this world as part of Satan's realm. Satan is the "strong man, fully armed" who is guarding "his own palace" and keeping "his goods in peace" (Luke 11:21).

We are all in that palace and among those goods! And there we would have stayed if it hadn't been for One who is stronger than the strong man. That, of course, is Jesus. He came to this earth to defeat the strong man, and He did that by dying on the cross. Paul points to Jesus' death as the defeat for Satan and his forces by writing of Christ and His cross: "Having disarmed principalities and powers, He made a public spectacle of them, triumphing over them in it" (Col. 2:15).

Although Satan has been defeated, he is not dead. So Jesus, our mighty warrior, defends us to the point that Satan will never be able to reclaim us (John 10:28).

Isaiah also proclaims the coming Christ as our "Everlasting Father." While Jesus is the Son, and not the Father, He has the same fatherly disposition as the Father. That disposition causes Him to care for the needs of His people. Fully aware of this, the Apostle Peter urged his readers to cast their cares upon the Lord with the confidence that He cared for them (1 Peter 5:7).

The word "Everlasting" assures us that Jesus' care isn't temporary. It's not here today and gone tomorrow. It never ends.

The prophet Isaiah has yet another name for the coming Christ—"Prince of Peace," or we might say "Peaceful Prince."

This title indicates both that Jesus would exhibit peace and produce peace. It's easy to see Jesus exhibiting peace. He never seemed to be upset, anxious, tense, or on edge. He lived such a peaceful life that He was able to say to His disciples: "Peace I leave with you, My peace I give to you; not as the world gives do I give to you" (John 14:27a).

Some look at all the wars and conflicts that have occurred since Jesus came, and conclude that He couldn't possibly be the Prince of Peace. The thing they fail to see is that the peace Jesus came to provide is peace with God. We can never have true peace with others until we have peace with God, and we can only have peace with God through Jesus.

Looking ahead to Christ, Isaiah said He "shall be called" these names. I'm a fulfillment of that prophecy. I call Jesus Wonderful Counselor, Mighty God, Everlasting Father, and Prince of Peace. I hope you do as well.

# -25-

## From God's Word, the Bible...

*"The LORD your God will raise up for you a Prophet like me from your midst, from your brethren. Him you shall hear. . . ."*

*"I will raise up for them a Prophet like you from among their brethren, and will put My words in His mouth, and He shall speak to them all that I command Him."*

*Deuteronomy 18:15,18*

# The Promise of a Prophet

Several titles come to mind when Moses' name is mentioned: deliverer, leader, warrior, mediator, lawgiver, and judge. One title that we don't seem to associate with Moses is prophet. But Moses was a prophet. He stood before Israel as God's man to declare God's truth.

For forty years, Moses had ably led Israel. Now he was preparing to step off the stage. As he did so, his mind was drawn to the coming Messiah. Moses declared that this coming One would be a prophet like unto himself. The New Testament pointedly declares Jesus to be the fulfilment of Moses' prophecy (Matt. 21:11; John 6:14; 7:40; Acts 3:22-23).

In what ways would Jesus be a prophet like Moses? First, as Moses was sent by God, so Jesus would be. As God raised up Moses, so He would raise up Jesus.

During His earthly ministry, Jesus emphasized that He came from God. This is especially prominent in John's Gospel (John 3:16-17; 5:24,30,36,38; 6:44,57; 7:16; 8:16,18; 9:4;

10:36; 11:42; 12:45,49; 14:24; 15:21; 16:5). Jesus also made it clear that He came from God to speak for God (John 8:38;14:10,24). That's what a prophet does. He speaks for God.

The words Jesus spoke were the words of God Himself! What Jesus had to say about the sinful nature of the human heart (Matt. 15:18-19), the certainty of divine judgment (John 5:22-30), and the terrible reality of hell (Matt. 23:33; Mark 9:42-48; Luke 16:19-31) is not merely another man sharing his opinions. It's nothing less than a divine message. And what Jesus had to say about eternal salvation through His own death on the cross is also divine (John 6:47-58).

Because these truths are divine, they are certain and imperishable. We can deny them, but we can't destroy them. The course of wisdom, then, is to both recognize that Jesus spoke the words of God, and humbly submit to them. It is to do nothing less than heed the words of Moses himself: "Him you shall hear" (v. 15).

The course of wisdom is to heed this word of warning from the Lord Himself: "And it shall be that whoever will not hear My word, which He speaks in My name, I will require it of him"(v. 18).

The Pharisees of Jesus' day refused to heed His words. To them Jesus said: "He who is of God hears God's words; therefore you do not hear, because you are not of God" (John 8:47).

Another way in which Jesus would be a prophet like Moses was in faithfulness. Moses wasn't perfect in faithfulness (Num. 20:1-13), but Jesus was. As God's Prophet, Jesus never failed to accurately declare the Word of God and never failed to live up to that word which he declared.

If Jesus had not been faithful to God in every respect, He would have been a sinner Himself and couldn't have paid for the sins of others. That's how very important it is!

A third way in which Jesus would be like Moses was that He would also arise from among the people (vv. 15,18).

The prophetic office Jesus came to discharge was mediatorial in nature. He came between the holy God and sinners to make peace. In this role, it was essential for Him to be able to fully represent both parties.

Since he was already God, there was no difficulty in Him representing God. In order to represent human beings, He had to be one, too. Here is the wonder and glory of the incarnation: Jesus added to His deity our humanity so that He was at one and the same time fully God and fully man.

He couldn't have done anything for us had He not been one of us. The author of Hebrews says of Christ: "Inasmuch then as the children have partaken of flesh and blood, He Himself likewise shared in the same. . ." (Heb. 2:14).

How gracious it was of God to send His Son to take up our humanity and in that humanity to speak to us the words of eternal life! We don't appreciate to a sufficient degree what God has done to provide salvation for us.

Sent by God! Faithful like Moses! Sent as one of us! What a prophet we have in Jesus! How we should prize His prophetic work! And we prize Him in that role only if we do as Moses said, that is, hear Him. We hear Him in the reading and faithful preaching, teaching, and application of His Word, the Bible.

# -26-

## From God's Word, the Bible...

*A bruised reed He will not break,*
*And smoking flax He will not quench;*
*He will bring forth justice for truth.*

Isaiah 42:3

# The Nature of Jesus

Do these verses from Isaiah really relate to the Lord Jesus Christ? The author of the first Gospel, Matthew, thought so and said so (Matt. 12:15-21). We surely wouldn't claim to know more about Jesus than one of His disciples.

Isaiah's prophecy deals with how Jesus would conduct His ministry. It must have been a precious blessing for its original readers, captives in distant Babylon. Their situation appeared to be so utterly hopeless. There seemed to be no future at all. But here was Isaiah affirming that there was a future. The Messiah would definitely come to the land of Israel, and would bring blessing both to Jews and Gentiles.

It had to be comforting to those captives to know that Christ would definitely come. It also had to be comforting to them to know that Christ would conduct Himself in a very comforting way. Isaiah's prophecy includes four blessed "nots."

The first "not" pertains to Jesus' manner of speaking:

> *He will not cry out, nor raise His voice. . . .*
> (v. 2a)

The Jews in Babylon were probably subjected to harsh speaking from their captors. The Messiah would treat His followers differently. Derek Thomas writes:

> Have you ever listened to a sergeant major drilling his men? Jesus never dealt with his disciples that way. There was no screaming or shouting of orders. He did not assume the role of a military commander.[2]

Tender gentleness would characterize Jesus and His ministry. Then we see two more "nots" in these words:

> *A bruised reed He will not break,*
> *And smoking flax He will not quench.*
> (v. 3)

The captives in Babylon also knew what it was like to be bruised reeds and smoking flax. The reed was a shoot from a plant that could be made into a musical instrument. It would work fine until it was cracked. Then there was nothing to do except break it and throw it away.

The smoking flax referred to a candle that was so close to going out that it was producing more smoke than light.

We can all identify with these images. They picture what life is often like for God's people. Life often pounds us so much that we feel as if we have no music or light left in us.

Have you ever noticed how some people enjoy making things worse for those who are beaten down by life? They seem to delight in breaking those who are bruised, and in stamping out those who are flickering.

The Lord Jesus isn't that way with His people. He doesn't break cracked reeds. He doesn't put out flickering candles.

---

[2] Derek Thomas, *God Delivers*, Evangelical Press, p. 281.

Far from it! He actually restores His beaten people so they can make music again and glow again.

If we could ask Simon Peter about this, He would take enormous delight in affirming it is so. After his three denials of Jesus, he must have felt as if he had no more usefulness than a bruised reed or a smoking candle. But the Lord Jesus found him and restored him (John 21).

Here's the final "not" Isaiah gives us about Jesus:

> *He will not fail nor be discouraged,*
> *Till He has established justice in the earth. . . .*
>
> (v. 4)

This means that the Lord Jesus would not fail to do the work that He would come to this earth to do. Part of that work, as we have been noting, was to comfort feeble people—Jesus Himself wouldn't be feeble in helping His feeble people. He wouldn't let anything throw Him off His course.

One way—the main way—Jesus would help feeble people would be the business of establishing justice in the earth.

By His death on the cross, the Lord Jesus answered the demands of God's justice on behalf of His people.

As a result of Jesus satisfying God's justice on their behalf, His people would have a love for God's law in their hearts and would seek to honor that law in their conduct. Because God's people will never be perfect in this life, God's justice will never be completely established in this world. But a new world is coming! In that world all wickedness will finally be banished, and God's justice will reign (Rev. 21:8,27).

While we wait for that world, the best thing we can do in this world is proclaim our tender, comforting Christ to hearts that ache from sin.

# -27-

## From God's Word, the Bible...

*My God, My God, why have You forsaken Me?*
*Why are You so far from helping Me,*
*And from the words of My groaning?*

*Psalm 22:1*

# Jesus Prophesies
the Cross

Of all the Old Testament prophecies about Jesus, the most detailed are Psalm 22 and Isaiah 53, and each chapter deals with the cross. That ought to underscore for us the importance of the cross, and it should be reason enough to devote one reading to each of these two splendid chapters.

One of the things that make Psalm 22 so remarkable is that it is the Messiah's own description of His crucifixion.

So the cross didn't take Jesus by surprise. He knew it was coming centuries before it came. This blows to smithereens the notion that Jesus came to this earth to set up an earthly kingdom only to have to fall back to Plan B, the cross, when the Jews rejected Him as their king.

The cross was never Plan B. The cross was in the mind and heart of God even before the world began. That's why the Bible calls Jesus "the Lamb slain from the foundation of the world" (Rev. 13:8).

How could God have planned the cross even before Adam and Eve fell into sin? The answer is that God knows the future as perfectly as He does the present or the past. Nothing ever catches Him off guard. He knew He would create this world, and He knew Adam would sin. So He had the cross ready before any of it occurred.

The fact that Jesus not only saw the cross coming but also saw the unspeakable agonies that He would have to endure there makes it all the more remarkable that He died there. He didn't have to. It was faithfulness to His Father and love for sinners that caused Him to relentlessly move toward the cross.

What were those unspeakable agonies that Jesus saw when He looked toward the cross? He mentions in this Psalm the cruel, vicious mockery that would be heaped on Him (vv. 6-8, see Matt. 27:41-43). He also mentions the thirst that He would have to endure, thirst so intense that His tongue would cling to His jaws (v. 15, see John 19:28).

The Messiah also mentions His garments being divided (v. 18), a prophecy that was minutely fulfilled (Matt. 27:35)

It's especially noteworthy that the Messiah used the word "pierced" in His description of the crucifixion. That word would become synonymous with crucifixion, but Psalm 22 was written centuries before crucifixion was ever practiced.

With the phrase "the night season" (v. 2), the Lord Jesus may very well have been anticipating the deep darkness that would fall over the land while He was on the cross (Matt. 27:45).

The greatest agony of the cross wouldn't be hearing the mockery, experiencing the thirst or seeing the soldiers dividing His garments. It wouldn't be the darkness. The greatest agony would be when Jesus, bearing the penalty for sinners, experienced in the place of those sinners the God-forsakenness that they deserve for their sins. Psalm 22 takes us to very heart of the cross in its very first words.

Yes, Jesus saw agony on the cross, and horrible agony it would be. But Jesus also saw victory, and the victory was such that it made the agony worthwhile.

Verse 21 brings us to a turning point in the psalm. The darkness lifts and the sunshine beams brightly. The storm of wrath has subsided, and all is peaceful and calm.

In the verses that remain, the Messiah rejoices that His death on the cross would not be in vain, but that it would achieve its purpose. He rejoices in the knowledge that "a posterity" will serve Him. Each generation will have those whom He purchased with His own blood to tell those in the generation following them of what He has done (vv. 30-31).

So Jesus wouldn't die on the cross with His fingers crossed, merely hoping that his death would accomplish something. That cross that He and the Father agreed upon before the world began would be effective in redeeming sinners.

As I read the Messiah's words in Psalm 22, I find myself saying with Horatius Bonar:

> *'Twas here the debt was paid—*
> *Hallelujah, hallelujah!*
> *Our sins on Jesus laid—*
> *Hallelujah, hallelujah!*
> *So round the cross we sing*
> *Of Christ our offering,*
> *Of Christ our living King—*
> *Hallelujah for the cross!*

# -28-

## From God's Word, the Bible...

*All we like sheep have gone astray;*
*We have turned, every one, to his own way;*
*And the LORD has laid on Him the iniquity of us all.*

*Isaiah 53:6*

# Christ, the Sin Bearer

Carried along by the Spirit of God, Isaiah saw the Lord Jesus dying on the cross, and he described what he saw in Isaiah 53. Amazingly enough, this was over 700 years before Jesus was born.

This chapter, long a favorite of the people of God, makes us wince and worship. We wince because the agony of the cross is so graphically described; and we worship because we realize that Jesus' death on the cross purchased for us forgiveness for our sins and right standing with God.

Each of the twelve verses of this chapter begs for substantial consideration, but the last sentence of the sixth verse seems to me to be the very apex of this temple of truth:

> And the LORD has laid on Him,
> the iniquity of us all.

There we have the nub of the matter. Jesus was on the cross in a substitutionary capacity. He was there in the place of sinners. He didn't have to be there, and once nailed to the cross, He didn't have to stay there. But He was there, and He stayed there to bear "the iniquity of us all."

The Bible uses various words to describe our condition—sin, wickedness, and transgression are words that come easily to mind. And yes, iniquity.

Iniquity! It's a foul, disgusting, revolting word. It's a nasty word to describe our nasty condition. Iniquity is twistedness. God made us a certain way, but sin has twisted us. We're not as God made us to be.

Sin is to sinful men and women a very simple thing. If God doesn't like our sin, He should just ignore it. He should just look the other way and act as if our sins don't even exist.

But what is simple to us is serious to God. The only thing that sinful men and women understand less than their sinful condition is the holiness of God. God is holy. That not only means that He is Himself free from all sin but also that He must judge our sin. For God to ignore our sin would amount to Him denying Himself. For God to ignore our sin would be equal to Him finding fault with Himself. He would be finding fault with His own holy character.

God's holiness demands that He both pronounce and carry out a just sentence upon sinners. There's no need to wait with bated breath for the sentence to be handed down. It is clearly stated in the Bible. It is everlasting separation from God. Many people say they can't understand such a harsh sentence. I can understand it. I can understand God looking upon the horror of sin and saying: "I'm not going to allow anything sinful to enter heaven. I'm not going to let sin do on the new earth what it did on the first earth."

So here we are in our sins, and here God is in His holiness! Is there any hope for us? Yes, the hope lies in the cross that Isaiah saw. That cross consisted of a special man dying a special death. When Jesus was on that cross, our sins were on Him. That's what Isaiah said to the people of faith in his day.

Jesus was on that cross as the sin-bearer. He had no sins of His own to pay for. So He could pay for the sins of others.

Unbelievers have no trouble coming up with questions. How could one man die for so many others? How could one man receive in the six hours that He was on the cross the penalty of eternal separation for our sins? The answer lies in those words "special man." Jesus wasn't a mere man; He was the God-man. So, in His death on the cross He could do things an ordinary man couldn't. As an infinite person, He could die for many others. As an infinite person, He could receive the infinite sentence of eternal wrath.

When I look at Isaiah 53, I see many important words, but I think the most precious words are the pronouns "our" and "us" and the preposition "for." It was "our griefs" and "our sorrows" that He carried with him to the cross. And it was "for our transgressions," "for our iniquities," and "for our peace" that he died (vv. 4-5). It was, my brother or sister in Christ, "the iniquity of us all" that was laid on Christ.

> *Bearing shame and scoffing rude*
> *In my place condemned he stood,*
> *Sealed my pardon with His blood;*
> *Hallelujah! what a Savior!*
> (Philip Bliss)

# -29-

## From God's Word, the Bible...

*Therefore my heart is glad, and my glory rejoices;*
*My flesh also will rest in hope.*
*For You will not leave my soul in Sheol,*
*Nor will You allow Your Holy One to see corruption.*
*You will show me the path of life;*
*In Your presence is fullness of joy;*
*At Your right hand are pleasures forevermore.*

*Psalm 16:9-11*

# The Resurrection of Jesus

Some of David's psalms consist of two tiers. One has to do with David himself and what he was experiencing at the moment. The other level, the higher level, has to do with the Lord Jesus Christ. So it is with Psalm 16. As we read it, we can see how it applied to David. But we also get the distinct impression that the psalm is not exclusively about him. While we hear David in these verses, we seem to hear another voice as well. We especially hear that voice in the last three verses of the psalm.

We get help from Peter and Paul on this matter of identifying the other voice. They insist that the Lord Jesus is speaking in Psalm 16:9-11, and He is speaking about a matter of utmost importance, that is, His resurrection (Acts 2:25-28; 13:35).

So these verses let us hear David expressing confidence that the grave wouldn't be the end for him, and, at the same time, they let us hear the Lord Jesus saying the same.

I wonder if Jesus had these words on His mind as He came down to death's door. I wonder if He said to Himself:

> *Therefore, my heart is glad, and my glory rejoices;*
> *My flesh also will rest in hope.*
> (v. 9)

We know that Jesus knew about His resurrection. He had predicted it on various occasions (e.g., Matt. 16:21; John 2:19-22). Jesus didn't descend into death with uncertainty and dread. The cross was something for Him to dread because it would mean being separated from God on behalf of sinners. But the grave -was not something for Him to dread. The grave was merely the passageway from death to life.

Jesus would die with a glad heart because He knew about His resurrection. He would die with His "glory" rejoicing. With everything that made Him the glorious person He was, that is with His whole being, He would rejoice in His soon-coming resurrection.

Isn't it staggering that in Psalm 16 we hear the Lord Jesus expressing confidence in His resurrection hundreds of years before He came to this earth?

His confidence wasn't ill-founded or misplaced. Jesus died and was buried. And on the third day, God raised Him up. The Father, being completely satisfied with what His Son had done on the cross, refused to leave His body "in Sheol," that is, in the realm of the dead. The Father refused to allow the body of His Son to "see corruption," that is, to rot away.

In nailing Him to the cross, sinful man spoke his "truth" about Jesus. In raising Him from the grave, God spoke His truth about Jesus, and His truth showed man's "truth" to be a complete lie. The cross was man's way of saying "Jesus is a fraud." The resurrection was the Father's way of saying "Jesus is God."

There are those who say that they would like to be sure that Jesus arose from the grave. How can they not be sure? The evidence is overwhelming. The heavy stone covering the tomb was rolled away. Angels were present. The Roman guards were in a stupor. The tomb was empty. The grave-clothes of Jesus were in a particularly convincing configuration. Many actually saw the risen Christ—over five hundred on one occasion (1 Cor. 15:6).

The problem with many people isn't that they can find no evidence to believe in Jesus' resurrection. It is rather that they don't want to believe the evidence because a risen Christ would put demands on them that they are unwilling to meet.

What a treasure we have in the closing verses of Psalm 16! Because Jesus spoke these words about His own resurrection, all who trust in Him as their Lord and Savior can speak them as well. So, in addition to hearing David and the Lord Jesus speak in these precious verses, I can hear yet another voice. It is my voice! Yes, I can go down to death's door with a glad heart and with my whole being rejoicing. I have the certainty that the grave is not my final home. This certainty is because Jesus said: "Because I live, you will live also" (John 14:19).

# -30-

## From God's Word, the Bible...

*You have ascended on high,*
*You have led captivity captive;*
*You have received gifts among men,*
*Even from the rebellious,*
*That the LORD God might dwell there.*

*Psalm 68:18*

# The Ascension of Jesus

We noted in the previous reading that some Old Testament passages move on two levels. One is the immediate level that relates to the author and what he was experiencing. The other is a higher level that finds fulfillment in the Lord Jesus Christ. It's the same with Psalm 68:18.

This sixty-eighth psalm pertains to warfare. This was something with which David was very familiar. Warfare in those days would often follow a pattern. Enemies would arise, the king of the nation would step down from his throne to lead in battle, the enemy would be defeated, captives would be taken, and the king would triumphantly return with those captives in tow to once again be seated on his throne. Furthermore, the king would often distribute the spoils of war to his subjects.

David himself followed this pattern on numerous occasions. But he also knew that there was more going on in his wars than men fighting men. Because Israel was the Lord's chosen nation, the Lord Himself would step down from His throne to defeat the enemies and triumphantly return with captives to take His throne. That's the reason the Psalm begins in this way:

> Let God arise,
> Let His enemies be scattered.

So the pattern we have here is coming, conquering, capturing, and conferring. The king would come to the battle, conquer and capture the enemy, and confer spoils on his people.

It's not surprising that Paul saw in David's pattern a picture of the ascension of the Lord Jesus Christ (Eph. 4:8-10). As David wrote Psalm 68:18, he himself may have also been enabled by God's Spirit to see the ascension of Jesus.

To say Jesus ascended to heaven is to say that He first descended from heaven. There was a time when the Lord Jesus rose from His throne to come to this earth. What brought Him to this earth? It was to engage in battle against the enemies of His people.

This battle took the Lord Jesus to the cross where He triumphed over Satan and his forces. Paul says of Jesus and His death on the cross: "Having disarmed principalities and powers, he made a public spectacle of them, triumphing over them in it" (Col. 2:15).

Jesus came and conquered. He came to this earth and conquered Satan just as God promised in Genesis 3:15. Matthew Henry puts it neatly, saying of Jesus: "He conquered those who had conquered us. . . ."

Having conquered, the Lord Jesus also took captives. He has "led captivity captive." Through His redeeming work on the cross, Jesus has taken all those who trust in Him out of their captivity to Satan and made them His own captives.

Many have a tendency to think that we are completely free. They like to think of themselves as standing between the Lord Jesus on one hand and Satan on the other. They tell us that they listened to the Lord Jesus state His case and then they listened to the devil state his case. Then they decided to choose Jesus, and He has been grateful to them ever since!

The Bible tells us that we always belong to a master. We are either in captivity to Satan or to Christ. When the Lord Jesus saves us, He takes us out of captivity to Satan and makes us His captives. But in wonderful irony, captivity to Christ makes us truly free (John 8:32). Ask a Christian if he is a captive, and he will say "Yes!" Ask him if he is free, and he will say "Yes!"

Because of His victory on the cross, the Lord Jesus has won spoils that He now lavishes on His people—marvelous privileges and advantages. He showers them with "every spiritual blessing" (Eph. 1:3).

Our need is to get a better understanding of Jesus' work on our behalf. He rose from His throne in glory to come down to this earth and even down to the grave itself so that He could take us out of captivity to Satan and make us His captives. After descending to this earth, Jesus ascended to heaven again (Acts 1:9-11). From there He pours out His gifts on His people.

We who have become His captives by His atoning death on the cross now glorify our ascended Christ who daily blesses us. And we look forward to that day when our ascended Lord will descend once more to take us to share His eternal glory.

# -31-

## From God's Word, the Bible...

*The LORD said to my Lord,*
*"Sit at My right hand,*
*Till I make Your enemies Your footstool."*
*The LORD shall send the rod of Your strength out of Zion.*
*Rule in the midst of Your enemies!*

*Psalm 110:1-2*

# The Gospel Reign
## of Jesus

No list of Old Testament prophecies of Christ is complete without Psalm 110, which is quoted more than any other in the New Testament.

I wonder what David was thinking as he wrote the words of verses 1 through 4. He had to know that they weren't just his words. He had to realize that he was being prompted to write words that were being given to him by God's Spirit. And what words! In these verses, David actually reports the words spoken by the Lord to the Lord!

Who are these Lords (v. 1)? The first is God the Father; the second is God the Son.

In the writing of this psalm, God's Spirit carried David all the way from the humiliation of Christ to His exaltation, that is, all the way from Jesus coming to this earth as a man to Him returning to heaven. The Spirit carries David from Jesus' descending to His ascending. Quite a tour!

What did David hear the Father saying to the Son? We

can capture it in the words "Sit" (v. 1), "Rule" (v. 2) and "You are" (v. 4).

The Father saying "Sit" to the Son would mean that redemption's work was now done. The agonies of the cross would be in the past. The grave would be defeated. With it all accomplished and over, the Father offers the Son the position of highest honor in heaven—the seat at His, the Father's, right hand.

The Father, fully satisfied with the redeeming work of His Son, has determined that He should have preeminence in all things (Col. 1:18).

If we want to be pleasing to God, we must seek to give Jesus the preeminence in our thinking, speaking, and doing. And we must give Him preeminence in our public worship. How sad it is that this needs to be said about worship, but our days make the saying of it essential.

With the word "Rule," the Father would be telling His Son to begin His gospel reign. We must not think that Jesus' rule is something that will occur at the end of time. Jesus is ruling now.

One of the things we need to note about this gospel reign is that it will finally result in the complete subjection of all the Messiah's enemies (v. 1). Every knee will finally bow before him and every tongue will finally confess that he is Lord (Phil. 2:9-11).

A second thing for us to note is that Jesus' reign is conquering enemies even now. As the church preaches the gospel, the Lord Jesus Christ extends his "rod" or scepter "out of Zion" (v. 2).

Here's another thing: Jesus' gospel reign is manifested by the people of God themselves. We don't have to be in the courts of heaven to see Jesus reigning. We see that reign every time a sinner is conquered by the gospel of Christ. How are sinners so conquered? By the Lord making them willing to receive the gospel! Thus the Father says to the Messiah:

> *Your people shall be volunteers*
> *In the day of Your power. . . .*
> (v. 3)

When the gospel exerts its conquering power, those who receive it begin to display "the beauties of holiness" (v. 3). Every sign of holiness among God's people is evidence that the gospel reign is in effect. That's no small thing because those saved in the gospel age will be as numerous as the drops of dew that come "from the womb of the morning" (v. 3).

With the words "You are," the Father accentuates the priestly work of King Jesus. The king is also a priest!

This dual role, as noted earlier in these readings, was pictured by Melchizedek, who was both a king and a priest in Abraham's day (Gen 14:18-20). While he was associated with both righteousness and peace, Melchizedek couldn't perfectly represent those things. But Jesus does.

The way by which he produced peace between guilty sinners and the holy God was through righteousness. He Himself lived a perfectly righteous life, providing the righteousness that we do not have, righteousness that is credited to us when we believe. Furthermore, Jesus' death also had to do with righteousness. He died to receive the righteous sentence of the holy God against our sins. In other words, He received on the cross what God's righteousness demanded, namely, the wrath of God.

David was certainly blessed to write these words, and we are certainly blessed to read them. And we are even more blessed if we find that we are truly subjects of the King, rescued from the power and dominion of sin, forever to love, serve, and obey Him. Is He your Lord and King?

# About the Author

Roger Ellsworth is a retired pastor, active in ministry and writing, who lives in Jackson, Tennessee. He and his wife, Sylvia, love the message of the Bible, and they enjoy sharing the wonderful counsel of the Word of God in language that ordinary people can understand and appreciate.

Roger has written numerous books on the Christian faith, and has exercised a preaching ministry for over fifty years. His sermons are available to listen for free on SermonAudio.com.

# The Series

*Enjoy collecting the My Coffee Cup Meditations Series.*

*A Dog and A Clock 978-0-9988812-9-4 (Series#1)*
*The "Thumbs-Up" Man 978-0-9988812-5-6 (Series#2)*
*When God Blocks Our Path 978-0-9988812-4-9 (Series#3)*
*Fading Lines, Unfading Hope 978-0-9996559-1-7 (Series#4)*
*The Day the Milk Spilled 978-0-9965168-6-0 (Series#5)*
*"Where Are the Donuts?" 978-0-9965168-7-7 (Series#6)*
*Sure Signs of Heavenly Hope 978-0-9988812-1-8 (Series#7)*
*My Dog Knows It's Sunday 978-0-9996559-6-2 (Series#8)*
*Rover and the Cows 978-0-9996559-7-9 (Series#9)*
*Apples of Gold in Silver Settings 978-0-9600203-0-0 (Series#10)*
*Old Houses, New Houses 978-0-9600203-1-7 (Series#11)*
*Golden Key and Silver Chain 978-0-9600203-2-4 (Series#12)*

Get the set for a special price:

www.mycoffeecupmeditations.com/crazyoffer

# Collect All the Books!

# MY COFFEE-CUP
## MEDITATIONS

www.mycoffeecupmeditations.com

CPSIA information can be obtained
at www.ICGtesting.com
Printed in the USA
LVHW050223201118
597697LV00008B/19

9 780960 020324